# HOME LOAN HACKS

**DAVE HIRST**

First published 2026 by Dave Hirst

Produced by Independent Ink



Cover design by Catucci Design
Edited by Daina Lindeman
Internal design by Independent Ink
Typeset in Montserrat by Post Pre-press Group, Brisbane
Cover image: Iryna Pasichnyk/istockphoto.com

NATIONAL LIBRARY OF AUSTRALIA
A catalogue record for this book is available from the National Library of Australia

ISBN 978-1-7647258-0-4 (paperback)
ISBN 978-1-7647258-1-1 (epub)
ISBN 978-1-7647258-2-8 (kindle)

*For Dad, Sonny and Stan.*
*The most positive people I know.*

# Contents

# Introduction

In March 2023, a TikTok video claiming to reveal a secret to paying no interest on a home loan went viral. The guy behind it – a laid-back Aussie in a sweat-stained T-shirt – looked convincing enough, with a fancy four-screen setup flashing colourful graphs and charts. His pitch? If you paid just $1 extra on your mortgage every day, the bank would stop charging you interest. Do this religiously, and – *boom* – you'd be debt-free faster than a crypto coin pumping to the moon.

Reality check: he was completely wrong. This so-called "hack" doesn't reset how interest is calculated. Paying an extra dollar a day WILL save you money (about $19 less interest per year on an average mortgage). Unless your mortgage balance is missing a few zeros, that's hardly going to let you retire early.

Naturally, the finance industry had a field day ripping this guy apart. Mortgage brokers (myself included) started getting calls from clients asking if they'd been missing out on some magic loop-hole. Some sheepishly admitted they doubted it would work but wanted to check just in case. Others decided to test it themselves, diligently adding an extra dollar per day, only to realise a month later that their interest charges looked ... exactly the same.

Soon enough, thousands of people had conducted their own experiments and reached the same conclusion: the guy was full of it.

Were the people who believed it gullible? Or just stupid?

Nope. Most were hardworking homeowners simply trying to get ahead. They weren't dumb – they were just unaware of how home loans actually work. And why wouldn't they be? Finance is dry, complex, and, let's be honest, boring as batshit.

Most people are as knowledgeable about home loans as I am about car engines. I can put fuel in, adjust the air-con, and maybe change a tyre if I absolutely have to. But beyond that? No idea. To me, mechanics are magicians when they diagnose an issue just by listening to the engine or tapping a random doodad under the bonnet.

To the machinic, though, tapping there is just the logical way to diagnose the problem. Years of working on cars have massively shrunk the complexity of an engine for a mechanic.

The more you know about something, the less complex it becomes.

Home loans are the same. They aren't actually that complicated, but if you don't understand them, they feel overwhelming. And that's exactly how the banks like it.

I know this because I've been there myself. Before I became a mortgage broker, I was just another homebuyer trying to figure this stuff out. I asked my bank manager a simple question about offset accounts, and he had no idea what I was talking about. That's when I realised the people selling us home loans don't always understand them themselves.

And when you don't understand something, you can fall for dodgy TikToks.

## This Book Is Different

If you've picked up this book, it's because you want to pay off your loan faster. Good news: you absolutely can. You just need to understand a few key things:

- How banks actually make money from your home loan (spoiler: it's not just interest rates).
- How interest is calculated and why the way you structure your loan matters.
- How to tweak your repayments to ensure more money goes toward paying off your debt, rather than lining the bank's pockets.
- How to use the available loan features strategically to reduce your interest bill.
- How minor adjustments – made consistently – can save you hundreds of thousands of dollars over the life of your loan.

No gimmicks. No "silver bullet" tricks. Just the real strategies that banks would rather you didn't know.

A home loan is the biggest financial commitment most of us will ever make. And yet, most borrowers feel powerless watching their bank balance drain every month, hoping they're making the right decisions. This book is here to change that.

## No, This Book Won't Make You Debt-Free by Christmas

If you're standing in a bookstore, flicking through this introduction, trying to decide whether to buy this book on the assumption it will reveal the "one trick" to clearing your mortgage in record time – put it down and head to the fantasy section.

There are no shortcuts. Anyone selling you a magical "hack" is a charlatan.

You've probably seen the ads.

> *"Banks don't want you to know this ..."*
> *"This one strategy could save you hundreds of thousands ..."*
> *"Register for our free webinar to learn the truth ..."*

And to be fair, the webinar usually starts well. There's some decent education in there.

But then something funny happens.

The "secret" never quite shows up.

Instead, you get the pitch:

> *"If you want the full strategy, it's inside our advanced program ..."*

Cue the $4,000 price tag.

And what they don't exactly highlight is that the end goal is often to guide you into buying an investment property, one that conveniently pays them a very healthy commission.

Now, there's nothing wrong with investing in property.

There *is* something wrong with dressing up a sales funnel as "education".

This book is the opposite of that.

No hidden upsells.

No withheld "advanced strategies".

No $4,000 paywall waiting at the end.

Everything I know about structuring your home loan, reducing interest, and paying off your loan faster is in this book.

No magic tricks.

No silver bullets.

Just strategies that actually work, explained in plain English.

So instead of spending thousands on a course and wondering what you're being sold, you can spend $29.95 on this book, learn how it all works, and make your own decisions without anyone trying to steer you into an overpriced property along the way.

Paying off your mortgage faster takes three things: knowledge, strategy, and a bit of discipline.

The good news? None of it is complicated.

If you're willing to put in a little effort, you can shave years off your loan and save tens – sometimes hundreds – of thousands of dollars along the way.

This book is designed to help you flip the script.

Because right now, your home loan is set up to work very well ... for the bank.

Let's change that.

## How This Book Is Laid Out

The book is broken into four parts:

### 1. The Problem

Most home loans are structured in a way that benefits the bank, not the borrower.

I'll show you exactly how, and why most people don't even realise it's happening.

### 2. The Maths

This is the part most people try to avoid … and it's also the most important.

If you want to win the game, you need to understand the rules.

I'll walk you through the key calculations (in plain English) so you can see how your loan actually works behind the scenes.

### 3. The Hacks

This is where things get practical.

Simple, effective strategies you can use to reduce interest and pay off your loan faster.

No magic tricks. No silver bullets. Just changes that actually move the needle.

### 4. Advanced Strategies

This is the stuff the "free seminars" love to tease.

Usually right before they try to sell you a property.

I'll break down the strategy properly, how it works, when it makes sense, and when it doesn't, so you can decide if it's right for you.

No sales pitch. No townhouse included.

## Disclaimer

This book is designed to explain home loans and debt reduction in a language you can actually understand. It's full of terrible dad jokes and cringey one-liners, but the way I see it, if you're cringing, at least you're still reading – and if you're still reading, you might actually learn something.

And if it sometimes feels like I'm talking directly to you—relax. That's not because I know anything about you. It's because rewriting the whole book to say "the borrower" instead of "you" would add about 7 extra letters every sentence, and frankly, life's too short for that.

Now, onto the important bit.

I'm not giving you personal advice.

For me to do that, I'd need to know a whole lot more about you – your income, your expenses, your goals, your debts, your risk tolerance, your favourite vegetable, and where you stand on the Neighbours vs Home and Away debate. I don't know any of that.

All I know is that you're holding this book. (Hopefully you paid for it.)

So here are the rules:

**1. This is general information only.**

Everything in this book is general in nature and does not take into account your personal objectives, financial situation or needs.

**2. You need to decide if it actually makes sense for you.**

Before acting on anything in this book, you should consider whether it's appropriate for your own situation.

**3. Talk to a professional before you do anything drastic.**

Home loan strategies can have significant financial, tax and legal implications. Before implementing anything you read here, you should seek advice from a qualified professional such as a mortgage broker, financial adviser, or accountant.

Also, a quick reality check: lending policies, interest rates, and tax laws change all the time. While every effort has been made to ensure the information in this book is accurate at the time of writing, things may have changed since then.

And finally, the legal bit: to the extent permitted by law, the author and publisher are not liable for any loss or damage arising from reliance on the information in this book.

# PART 1

# THE PROBLEM

**IN THIS SECTION, YOU'LL LEARN:**

How the banks are very good at making money.

That the banks' goals are usually very different to your goals.

How not all accounts are created equal.

The importance of compounding.

## CHAPTER ONE

# Your Goals vs Bank Goals

Aussie banks: Good businesses. Definitely not charities.

Banks make billions of dollars in profit every year. In the 2025 financial year, just the big four banks made a combined net profit of $29.8 billion.*

That's profit.

After expenses.

After wages.

After keeping the lights on.

Now, the word billion gets thrown around so casually these days it barely registers. It's one of those numbers your brain nods at politely before wandering off to think about lunch.

So, let's translate it into human.

A billion isn't a slightly bigger million.

It's one thousand lots of one million.

* https://kpmg.com/au/en/insights/industry/australian-big-4-major-banks-full-year-results-2024.html

If you earned $1 million a year – and somehow managed not to spend a cent on food, housing, or the occasional will-to-live purchase – it would take you close to 30,000 years to earn what those four banks made in one year.

By the time you got there, interest rates would probably still be "about to rise".

Another way of looking at it is that the big four banks made a $95 profit per second.

PER SECOND!

And that's not just over the eight hours of the business day. They made $95 per second every single second of every minute of every hour of every day for the whole year. Weekends, holidays, and gluttony-fuelled sickies included.

This doesn't mean banks are evil. It just means their priorities may not always align with yours. Their goal is to keep your loan running as long as possible, while your goal should be to pay it off as quickly as possible. Understanding this difference is key to making sure you're structuring your loan in a way that benefits you – not them.

## Where Do the Bank's Profits Come From?

That $29.8 billion doesn't appear out of thin air – it comes from interest charges, fees, and the way loans are structured to maximise revenue.

Here's an example:

Let's say you take out a $500,000 home loan at 6% interest over 30 years. The bank will happily tell you your monthly repayment is $2,997 – which sounds manageable. But what they don't highlight is that over 30 years, you will actually pay back a staggering $1,079,000.

Yes, you read that right. You borrowed $500,000, but by the time you're done, you'll have paid more than double that amount – with the extra $579,000 going straight to the bank in interest.

And here's the kicker: most of this interest is front-loaded in the first few years of the loan. That's why, when you check your mortgage balance after five years of faithfully making repayments, it feels like you've barely made a dent.

If you've ever felt like your mortgage isn't shrinking, despite making payments month after month – you're not alone. Many borrowers experience this frustration, and it's not because they're doing anything wrong. It's because the system is designed that way.

## Top-Shelf vs Bottom-Shelf Lending

Given what we now know about how banks make their money – and how their advice is shaped by what makes them money – it's no wonder most Aussies end up with a home loan that benefits the bank far more than it benefits them.

There's an old idea called the "boots theory". Terry Pratchett coined it. He said that a rich man buys a $100 pair of boots that lasts ten years. A poor man buys a $20 pair of boots that wear out in one year. But over ten years, the poor man ends up spending $200 on boots – and still has wet feet.

Why? Because he couldn't afford the good boots up front. He didn't have the cash – or the knowledge – to buy better boots. As a person of limited means, he defaulted to the affordable option without even considering the one that he was told was more expensive.

Banks apply this same logic to home loans.

When you walk into a bank and ask for a loan, they'll offer you the bottom-shelf option – the loan that looks cheap, sounds simple, and has a low interest rate slapped on the front like a shiny price tag. But it's the "cheap boots" of banking. It wears out your finances over time. It gives the bank the best margin. It keeps you locked in for longer, paying more interest, with fewer features that actually help you.

Now, they do have the good boots in stock – better loans, smarter structures, features like offset accounts or flexible repayment options that could help you smash your loan faster and save a fortune in interest.

But they won't recommend those unless you ask for them.

And you won't ask for them if you don't know they exist.

So, unless you understand how home loans work and what to ask for, you'll probably walk out with the financial equivalent of cheap boots. And just like the poor bloke with wet socks, you'll end up paying more in the long run.

The less you know, the more they earn.

## How Small Tweaks Can Save You Thousands

Let's go back to that $500,000 loan over 30 years at 6%, and employ the two most basic home loan hacks.

**HACK #1**

***Pay more regularly (than monthly).***

If you simply make fortnightly repayments instead of monthly, you'll cut around five and a half years off your loan and save over $120,000 in interest over the life of the loan.

## HACK #2

*Pay more than the minimum.*

If you increase your repayment by just $50 per fortnight, you'll save another $40,000 in interest and clear your loan even faster. That's the power of small tweaks.

It's not about magic tricks or gimmicks – it's about understanding how loans work and leveraging that knowledge to pay less in interest and become debt-free sooner.

So, what does this mean for you as a borrower? It means that every piece of advice your bank gives you might not be in your best financial interest. Not because they're trying to trap you in debt, but because they are offering you the most profitable option for them.

To win at the mortgage game, you have to know which loan features will save you money and how to structure your cash flow in a way that benefits YOU – not them.

The good news? You don't have to follow the bank's plan. You have the power to take control of your loan, make it work for you, and save yourself years of unnecessary interest payments. The next few chapters will show you exactly how to do that. So, are you ready to start playing the game on your terms?

CHAPTER TWO

# A Word of Warning

## The 30-Year Steam Train

There will be maths.

I would love to use engaging stories and humorous examples to explain how loans work and avoid using maths altogether, but that is simply not going to happen. The following chapters are going to include a fair whack of calculations, equations, and tables. My job is to explain and interpret them for you without reverting to my native Nerdlish.

But you are going to have to meet me halfway. You're going to need to learn and understand some of the lingo we use to describe finance, as there is just no other way to describe these concepts. Don't worry – I'm going to translate them into normal English, and there's even a glossary at the back of the book that you can refer to if you forget the meaning of something you've already read.

The upside of this is that you will know your shit. You won't sound like a fresh fish when you walk into your bank to demand a better deal on your home loan. You'll also impress easily impressed people at BBQs, and it's possible that your newfound knowledge of all things finance could mean the difference between winning the bar tab or the stubby cooler at the local trivia night.

And honestly, it's not that hard. My favourite subject at school was history, and I did what other students called "Maths in Space", which relates less to the kind of math you would need to go into space and more to the spaced-out kids in the class.

At university, my passion was Asian languages. After uni, I became a teacher of the English language, and it wasn't until my early 30s that I found an interest in finance. If this Arts student can grasp the concept of compound interest, then so can you.

You can do it.

Pep talk over.

## A Typical Aussie Loan

The following few pages describe how the typical Aussie moves their money around, and how it really doesn't do them any favours. This is the reality check part of the book.

If we are looking at The Good, The Bad, and The Ugly, this section is about The Bad and Ugly.

The rest of the book goes into more detail about home loan hacks, so we can minimise some of The Bad and Ugly aspects of home loans and increase The Good.

## The Bad and The Ugly

Most Australians are on crap loans. Actually, that's not quite true. Many are on perfectly good loans, but aren't using the features of the loan in a way that benefits them. Many others are, indeed, on crap loans.

Most borrowers are on a standard variable rate loan, a fixed rate loan, a basic home loan, or a variation of these. They work in much the same way as any other loan.

It starts with the reward for your hard work (wages) getting deposited into your daily account. Once a month, your home loan repayment is automatically taken from there in much the same way that your phone bill or health insurance premium might be. Let's have a really simple look at this structure.

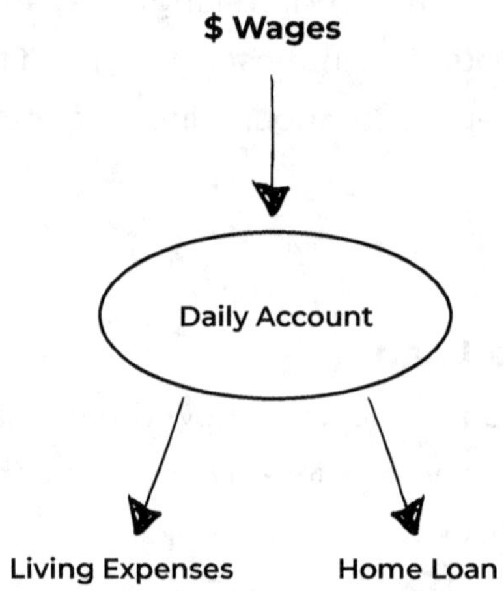


## Daily Account

Income goes into the daily account, where it waits patiently until it is spent. The home loan repayment comes out of here, and until the next pay is deposited, the balance of the daily account gradually (or rapidly) dwindles as bills are paid and groceries and fuel are purchased.

### Home Loan

Most loans are what we call P&I – principal and interest. You pay a certain amount each month, and this covers the entire interest cost, plus a little bit more to chip away at the actual loan – the principal. How the banks work out what your monthly payment needs to be to retire your debt in exactly 30 years is really complicated. It's called amortisation, and I promise that I am not going to bore you with it. You can check out the explanation of amortisation in the glossary if you don't have a life.

## So, My Loan Will Cost Me How Much?

A $500,000 loan at 6% interest over 30 years (and for the sake of simplicity, we are assuming your loan has no fees) would need to have a monthly P&I payment of $2,998 in order to go from a balance of $500,000 in Month 1 to a $0 balance at the end of Month 360 (30 years later).

I'm going to explain interest calculations in a lot more detail later on, so the following is just a taste tester of the super-exciting content that I know you just cannot wait to dig your teeth into.

We are going to start with a big-picture view of a typical home loan and then drill down to the specifics as we go on.

If you make your repayments monthly, then your loan balance is not going to change for the whole month. At the end of the month (usually the monthly anniversary of the settlement of your loan), your repayment is automatically pulled from your savings account and deposited into your home loan. Unfortunately, you're not allowed even a second to admire your new home loan balance, as the bank then promptly collects its monthly interest, bumping your loan back up again. This is how it looks:

| Opening Balance | $500,000 |
|---|---|
| Monthly Payment | - $2,998 |
| New Balance | $497,002 |
| Monthly Interest | + $2,500 |
| Closing Balance | $499,502 |

You paid $2,998 of your money into the loan, and then the bank takes $2,500 of it straight out, so you've only reduced your debt by $498.

Look at it this way. You borrowed $500,000 to buy your home. In the first month, you paid off $498 of that $500,000 and also paid $2,500 to the bank as a thank you for lending you the dough.

In the next month, you pay another $2,998, and once again, the bank takes the interest that is owed to them.

| Opening Balance | $499,502 |
|---|---|
| Monthly Payment | - $2,998 |
| New Balance | $496,504 |
| Monthly Interest | + $2,500 |
| Closing Balance | $499,004 |

Two months into your 360-month home loan, you've coughed up $5,996 of your money, and your loan has not even reduced by a grand.

Scary, huh? And this is just after two months. What does it look like after two years? Ten years? Thirty years? Now, I don't mean to depress you, but here's a few numbers to digest:

## Running Balances

| Age of loan | Your money paid to the bank | Loan reduced by |
|---|---|---|
| 6 months | $17,988 | $3,149 |
| 1 year | $35,976 | $6,145 |
| 2 years | $71,952 | $12,669 |
| 5 years | $179,880 | $35,668 |
| 10 years | $359,760 | $81,430 |
| 15 years | $539,640 | $144,509 |
| 20 years | $719,520 | $229,549 |
| 25 years | $899,400 | $344,345 |
| 30 years | $1,079,280 | $500,000 |

That's right. A $500,000 loan paid off over 30 years at 6% will end up costing you over DOUBLE the original loan amount. And don't forget we are assuming your loan has no fees, so in reality, it's probably even more.

Of course, this is very unrealistic because it assumes that the interest rate never changes over the entire 30-year period. If the rate is sometimes lower than 6% and sometimes higher than 6%, then it might not be drastically out.

Let's go back and have a look at just the first two months again, because this is where interest gets scary. If you thought paying interest on your loan was bad enough, how would you feel about paying interest on the interest that you have already paid?

At the end of the first month, the interest is added onto the loan balance, so the opening balance in Month 2 includes the interest from Month 1.

| | | |
|---|---|---|
| **Month 1** | Opening Balance | $500,000 |
| | Monthly Payment | - $2,998 |
| | New Balance | $497,002 |
| | Monthly Interest | + $2,500 |
| | Closing Balance | $499,502 |
| **Month 2** | Opening Balance | $499,502 |
| | Monthly Payment | - $2,998 |
| | New Balance | $496,504 |
| | Monthly Interest | + $2,500 |
| | Closing Balance | $499,004 |

*The opening balance of Month 2 includes the interest cost of Month 1*

The interest you pay becomes part of your balance each month before the next round of interest is calculated. So, in Month 2, you're charged interest on your Month 1 interest.

By Month 3? You're paying interest on the interest on the interest.

This is why paying off your loan feels like you're walking on an airport travelator going in the wrong direction and tilted slightly uphill. You take two steps forward and the travelator moves you one-and-three-quarters steps back. You never seem to be getting anywhere, because the interest compounds every month – just not in your favour.

How do banks pull this off? Easy. They design the system so your money sits in accounts that work for them.

## CHAPTER THREE

# Not All Accounts Were Created Equal

### Savings Accounts

Where does your pay go? For most people, it lands in a transaction or savings account earning 0% interest. Park $1,000 in this account and wait a year, and the bank will reward you with precisely $0 of interest earned.

When the ATM spits out your balance, it calls it your "Available Balance", not your savings.

Available. To spend. Immediately. Preferably on things that keep you broke.

Meanwhile, the bank uses *your* money to fund loans and collect interest from *other* customers. And they might still charge *you* an account-keeping fee for the privilege.

Solution? High-interest online savings account, right?

## High-Interest Accounts

Park your money in here, and you'll earn interest on it. It will be almost nothing, but, hey, it is better than 0%. You might even go for a term deposit that pays a slightly higher interest rate fixed for a certain period of time. The interest you earn in a high-interest online account or term deposit is higher than that of the basic transaction account, but is always lower than the home loan interest rate. How would the banks profit from your deposits otherwise?

So, if the home loan rate is, say 6%, then a good online account might be paying you 4% interest. Park $1,000 in there and don't touch it for a year, and hey presto, you now have $1,040 after the 4% interest is paid.

Slow down. Before you rush out and live like a king for several seconds, remember that not all of that $40 interest windfall is yours. Nope, the government will want to take their cut as well. Whenever you earn money – whether it be through wages, the sale of an investment, or interest in a savings account – you're supposed to pay tax on it. This funds our schools, hospitals, roads, and some of the best-paid politicians in the world.

For the time being, I'm going to spare you an explanation of the marginal tax system in Australia. But fear not, later on, I will regale you with possibly the dullest section of the book.

In short, how much tax you pay boils down to how much you earn, so in theory, if you earn more, you pay a larger proportion of your income in tax. For ease of explanation, let's just assume that you pay roughly 30% of your income in tax.

Now, 30% of $40 is $12, so you are left with $28 that you are now free to go and use to fund the extravagant lifestyle that such money brings. After tax, that 4% high-interest online savings account is actually only paying you 2.8%.

### *Inflation*

Inflation is simply the rate at which goods and services increase in value or cost. So, what you buy for $1,000 today might cost you more than that in the future.

Let's say that your $1,000 savings could buy you exactly one doodad today. You are really tempted to buy that doodad, as only cool people have them, and it's going to come in super handy when you go to the doodad festival next year.

But instead of buying the doodad now, you choose to invest your $1,000 in the high-interest online account paying 4%. One year later, you have $1,028 after tax is taken out. Off you trot to the doodad shop, only to find out that they now cost $1,050.

This is inflation, and it has killed the miserable after-tax interest you earned on your account, and then some.

Not only are high-interest online accounts not the prolific money earners that people think they are once tax and inflation come into play, most banks seem to discourage people from parking money in these accounts. Think about it. From the bank's perspective, where would they rather you park your money? In an account they pay you 0% interest on, or in an account they pay you 4% interest on?

Most banks, therefore, place restrictions on their high-interest accounts. For example, very few of them are transactional. This means you don't have an ATM card for the account, and you can't pay bills from it either. If you want some of the money, you need to transfer it to your 0% transaction account and withdraw the cash or pay the bill from there. As this is a bit of a hassle, most people only transfer the money they don't need into the high-interest account, leaving the bulk of their income in the 0% account, ready to pay for their living expenses.

Some banks also set minimum withdrawal amounts. If you only need $100 from the high-interest account, they might make you transfer $500 as a minimum, hoping that you're too lazy to transfer the $400 that you don't need back into it.

These are just a couple of examples of how the banks influence where you park your cash.

## Your Other Accounts

Aside from the account that you have your income getting paid into, what other accounts do you have? Do you have multiple accounts that are for different purposes? Bills account, holiday account, Christmas account, kids savings account, etc. Are these 0% transaction accounts, or are you earning interest on them?

How about the other accounts that you have that are not assets? Cash in the bank is an asset. It is something of value that you own, and it is also hopefully providing you with an income.

The other side of the coin is liabilities. These are things that cost you money. Things like personal loans, credit cards, and home loans are liabilities. You might have used the funds from these loans to buy an asset, but the account itself is not an asset.

### *Asset or Liability?*

An asset is usually described in the financial world as something that either provides you with an income or that you could sell for more than what you bought it for.

A liability is something that costs you money while you own it and generally does not increase in value over time.

Money sitting in a high-interest online savings account is an asset as you are earning interest on the deposit.

An investment property is an asset as it earns you an income in the form of rent, and ideally, you would be able to sell it for more than you bought it for, while getting some sweet taxation benefits while you own it.

That surfing trip to Indo may have been awesome for your mental health, but if you can't sell it to someone else and get the money you paid for it and more back, then it is not an asset.

How about your car? Unless you have a rare collector's item of a vehicle, your car is not really an asset either. In fact, it's probably a liability. It costs money to run and service, and it falls in value rapidly.

The most common liabilities are bank debts – personal loans, credit cards, and home loans. The loans themselves do not provide you with a financial benefit in the form of income or capital growth. Instead, they cost you money each and every month until the loan is paid off.

In almost all cases, liabilities attract a higher interest rate than assets. Your home loan interest rate is almost guaranteed to be higher than the high-interest savings account's interest rate. Personal loans are higher again, and credit cards top the list with rates between 10% and 25%.

## False Savings vs Real Savings

I've seen hundreds of cases of false savings. This happens when people keep money in an account that pays a low level of interest, while they slave away with payments to a liability with a very high interest rate.

In one example, I had a client who wanted to get a better deal on his home loan and was very proud of the $35,000 he had saved up in his ING Savings Maximiser account. At the time, this account was paying him about 2% after tax, but at the same time, he had a home loan with an interest rate of 4.8% and a credit card with $15,000 owing that was beating him over the head with a whopping 21% interest rate.

### False Savings

***Asset***

| Type | Balance | Interest Rate | Annual Earnings |
|---|---|---|---|
| Savings | $35,000 | 2% | $700 |

***Liability***

| Type | Balance | Interest Rate | Annual Cost |
|---|---|---|---|
| Credit Card | $15,000 | 21% | $3,150 |

**Net Position: $2,450 cost per year.**

He was earning $700 a year on the savings at 2%, but four times this amount was getting swallowed by the credit card interest, which was costing him $3,150 per year. He would have been much better off using $15,000 of the savings to pay off the credit card (then cut it up) and just leaving the remaining $20,000 in the savings account. This would have reduced the interest he was earning to $400 per year, but he would be saving another $3,150 on the credit card that he could then use to boost his savings even faster.

### Real Savings

*Asset*

| Type | Balance | Interest Rate | Annual Earnings |
|---|---|---|---|
| Savings | $20,000 | 2% | $400 |

*Liability*

| Type | Balance | Interest Rate | Annual Cost |
|---|---|---|---|
| Credit Card | $0 | 21% | $0 |

**Net Position: $400 earnings per year.**

**Difference: $2,850 better off each year by using savings to pay off debt.**

I get why people do this. Psychologically, having money in the bank can be a massive motivator for some people. But looking at it logically, taking all the emotion out of it and purely doing the maths, only the bank benefits from false savings such as this.

So, what are you doing? What accounts do you have, and where do you park your money? If you are earning interest, how much are you earning, and what does that work out to be after tax? What liabilities do you have, and what interest are you paying on these?

I strongly recommend drawing a mud map of your accounts so you can get a visual idea of how your money moves around, which accounts it sits in, and whether you earn or pay interest on those accounts.

## SUMMARY

Most Australians are moving their money around in a way that benefits the banks.

This means they are earning no or low interest on their savings but paying high interest on their liabilities.

This creates a false saving and means the banks earn more interest on our debts while paying us less interest on our savings.

Allowing the banks to set up your accounts is like asking a fast-food company for a diet plan.

How do we turn this around?

First, we need to understand one thing properly.

Interest.

How interest is calculated is THE most important equation in finance.

# PART 2

# THE MATHS

**IN THIS SECTION, YOU'LL LEARN:**

How interest is calculated on your home loan, and why this is the most important calculation to understand.

Why you'll pay more interest in some months and less in others.

Why the length of the loan is sometimes more important than the interest rate.

CHAPTER FOUR

# Calculating Interest

## Kill the Ostrich and Eat the Frog

We've all heard the myth that ostriches bury their heads in the sand when faced with danger. The idea goes that the ostrich is so dumb that it thinks if it can't see the predator rapidly approaching, then the predator will not be able to see it either.

If this actually did happen, I'm pretty sure ostriches would have gone the way of the dodo by now.

Though the myth is a work of fiction, its lesson is that we humans are often guilty of acting like the ostrich by avoiding important news that is inconvenient or potentially dangerous.

Economists at a US college conducted a study in 2013 that revealed college students would actually pay to avoid getting bad news about their health. They recruited students to participate in a study that required them to provide a blood sample to be used in a range of tests. Students were assured the study was completely free and 100% confidential.

They were then shown a range of ailments that the tests would be looking for. Chief among them were the two main variants of herpes, oral and genital, with the latter being a common STD that many adventurous college students contract as part of their extracurricular activities.

The nervous participants were then given the option of opting out of being told the results of some of the tests. Surprisingly, 5.2% decided to be kept in the dark on their results in the oral herpes test. A whopping 15.6% bailed on finding out if they had genital herpes, despite the fact their blood was going to be drawn and the tests run anyway, the process was completely free, and confidentiality was guaranteed.

It gets better. Those who declined the herpes test even paid $10 to NOT find out if they had it!*

This is called the "ostrich effect". And it shows up everywhere in financial behaviour. People don't open bills. Investors avoid checking their portfolios when the market drops. And homeowners? Many don't learn how their loan actually works – even though doing so could save them tens or hundreds of thousands of dollars.

Which brings us to frogs.

Mark Twain allegedly said, "Eat a live frog first thing in the morning and nothing worse will happen to you all day." The frog represents your hardest task – the thing you're most likely to procrastinate on, but that will help you most.

Learning how interest works on your home loan? That's the frog.

So, let's kill the ostrich, eat the frog, and take the first step to mastering your mortgage.

* https://papers.ssrn.com/sol3/papers.cfm?abstract_id=2370983

## How Interest Is Calculated

This is the most important part of this book.

The following pages are vital to taking control of your debt. Yes, it involves maths. And, no, it's not as painful as you think. If you own a home or ever plan to, this chapter is a must-read. It's the secret sauce behind every home loan hack in this book.

My opinion – if you have a home loan, you NEED to understand how interest is calculated.

Do a couple of star jumps, crack your neck, and get a triple-shot espresso to go. You'll need it.

## Interest vs Repayments

Your mortgage repayment has two components:

- Principal: the amount you borrowed.
- Interest: the bank's cut for lending it to you.

When you see headlines like "You'll pay $520,000 in interest on a $500,000 loan", they're talking about this second part. Over 30 years, interest adds up. A lot.

But here's where most people misunderstand what's happening.

When someone says, "I'm on 6%," that's the annual interest rate.

So, if you've got a $500,000 loan at 6%, it's tempting to think:

$$\$500{,}000 \times 6\% = \$30{,}000 \text{ per year}$$

$$\$30{,}000 \div 12 = \$2{,}500 \text{ per month}$$

Nice and neat.

And wrong.

Close ... but wrong.

## The Rule You Actually Need to Know

Interest is:

- Quoted annually.
- Charged monthly.
- Calculated daily.

That last part is the game changer.

Banks don't calculate your interest once a month. They calculate it every single day.

Here's the real formula:

$$\frac{(\text{Principal} \times \text{Annual Interest Rate})}{365}$$

That gives you your daily interest cost.

Let's plug in the numbers.

$$\$500{,}000 \times 6\% = \$30{,}000 \text{ per year}$$
$$\$30{,}000 \div 365 = \$82.19 \text{ per day}$$

That's the number that matters.

If you owe $500,000 at 6%, you are paying the bank:

$82.19 every single day.

Weekends included.

Public holidays included.

Christmas Day included.

That's the cost of carrying the debt.

CHAPTER FIVE

# The Variables That Change Everything

At the end of the month, the bank simply adds up all those daily amounts.

| Date | Loan Day of the Month | Loan Balance | Annual Interest Rate | Daily Interest |
|---|---|---|---|---|
| 15 January | 1 | $500,000 | 6% | $82.19 |
| 16 January | 2 | $500,000 | 6% | $82.19 |
| 17 January | 3 | $500,000 | 6% | $82.19 |
| 18 January | 4 | $500,000 | 6% | $82.19 |
| 19 January | 5 | $500,000 | 6% | $82.19 |
| 20 January | 6 | $500,000 | 6% | $82.19 |
| 21 January | 7 | $500,000 | 6% | $82.19 |
| 22 January | 8 | $500,000 | 6% | $82.19 |
| 23 January | 9 | $500,000 | 6% | $82.19 |

| Date | Loan Day of the Month | Loan Balance | Annual Interest Rate | Daily Interest |
|---|---|---|---|---|
| 24 January | 10 | $500,000 | 6% | $82.19 |
| 25 January | 11 | $500,000 | 6% | $82.19 |
| 26 January | 12 | $500,000 | 6% | $82.19 |
| 27 January | 13 | $500,000 | 6% | $82.19 |
| 28 January | 14 | $500,000 | 6% | $82.19 |
| 29 January | 15 | $500,000 | 6% | $82.19 |
| 30 January | 16 | $500,000 | 6% | $82.19 |
| 31 January | 17 | $500,000 | 6% | $82.19 |
| 01 February | 18 | $500,000 | 6% | $82.19 |
| 02 February | 19 | $500,000 | 6% | $82.19 |
| 03 February | 20 | $500,000 | 6% | $82.19 |
| 04 February | 21 | $500,000 | 6% | $82.19 |
| 05 February | 22 | $500,000 | 6% | $82.19 |
| 06 February | 23 | $500,000 | 6% | $82.19 |
| 07 February | 24 | $500,000 | 6% | $82.19 |
| 08 February | 25 | $500,000 | 6% | $82.19 |
| 09 February | 26 | $500,000 | 6% | $82.19 |
| 10 February | 27 | $500,000 | 6% | $82.19 |
| 11 February | 28 | $500,000 | 6% | $82.19 |
| 12 February | 29 | $500,000 | 6% | $82.19 |
| 13 February | 30 | $500,000 | 6% | $82.19 |
| 14 February | 31 | $500,000 | 6% | $82.19 |
| | | | **Total** | **$2,547.89** |

If there are 31 days in your loan month, you'll pay 31 days' worth of interest.

If there are 30, you'll pay 30.

If February rolls around, you'll pay less.

That's why your interest charge zig-zags slightly each month. But that's not the important bit.

## Which Variables Matter?

The interest you pay each month depends on three things:

1. Your loan balance.
2. Your interest rate.
3. The number of days in the month.

Reduce **ANY** of these variables, and you will reduce the amount of interest that you pay for that month.

## Which of these do you have control over?

Number of days in the month or year? I'm pretty sure that changing the Gregorian calendar is going to be beyond even your amazing abilities.

Reducing your interest rate? Yep, and this is why you should review your home loan on an annual basis. But this is not something that we have a lot of control over. We can't demand that the bank drop the interest rate to one that we feel is fair. And changing loans every time another bank comes out with a slightly lower rate is going to end up costing you more than you will save.

And that leaves ... your loan balance. No, we can't just choose to conveniently reduce it to $0, but this is the variable that we have the most control over.

Every hack in this book is built on one simple principle:

**Reduce the balance of the loan as early as possible to reduce the amount of interest you pay.**

That's it.

No magic.

No conspiracy.

Just maths.

And now you understand it.

| Date | Loan Day of the Month | Loan Balance | Annual Interest Rate | Daily Interest |
|---|---|---|---|---|
| 15 January | 1 | $500,000 | 6% | $82.19 |
| 16 January | 2 | $500,000 | 6% | $82.19 |
| 17 January | 3 | $500,000 | 6% | $82.19 |
| 18 January | 4 | $500,000 | 6% | $82.19 |
| 19 January | 5 | $500,000 | 6% | $82.19 |
| 20 January | 6 | $500,000 | 6% | $82.19 |
| 21 January | 7 | $500,000 | 6% | $82.19 |
| 22 January | 8 | $500,000 | 6% | $82.19 |
| 23 January | 9 | $500,000 | 6% | $82.19 |
| 24 January | 10 | $500,000 | 6% | $82.19 |
| 25 January | 11 | $500,000 | 6% | $82.19 |
| 26 January | 12 | $500,000 | 6% | $82.19 |
| 27 January | 13 | $500,000 | 6% | $82.19 |
| 28 January | 14 | $500,000 | 6% | $82.19 |
| 29 January | 15 | $500,000 | 6% | $82.19 |
| 30 January | 16 | $500,000 | 6% | $82.19 |
| 31 January | 17 | $500,000 | 6% | $82.19 |

| Date | Loan Day of the Month | Loan Balance | Annual Interest Rate | Daily Interest |
|---|---|---|---|---|
| 01 February | 18 | $500,000 | 6% | $82.19 |
| 02 February | 19 | $500,000 | 6% | $82.19 |
| 03 February | 20 | $500,000 | 6% | $82.19 |
| 04 February | 21 | $500,000 | 6% | $82.19 |
| 05 February | 22 | $500,000 | 6% | $82.19 |
| 06 February | 23 | $500,000 | 6% | $82.19 |
| 07 February | 24 | $500,000 | 6% | $82.19 |
| 08 February | 25 | $500,000 | 6% | $82.19 |
| 09 February | 26 | $500,000 | 6% | $82.19 |
| 10 February | 27 | $500,000 | 6% | $82.19 |
| 11 February | 28 | $500,000 | 6% | $82.19 |
| 12 February | 29 | $500,000 | 6% | $82.19 |
| 13 February | 30 | $500,000 | 6% | $82.19 |
| 14 February | 31 | $500,000 | 6% | $82.19 |
| | | | **Total** | **$2,547.89** |

CHAPTER SIX

# Why the Interest Rate Is Not the Be-All and End-All

So now you know how interest is calculated. But it's what happens next that is the cherry on the cake for the banks. Because not only do they calculate interest on the balance of the loan that you owe them, they also calculate interest on the interest that you've already paid. Genius.

## Exponential Growth and Compound Interest

If you've ever listened to Tony Robbins, the most famous of the personal improvement speakers, you've probably heard his golf analogy. I'll give you the short version, but if you have time, check out a video of it.*

Two friends – let's call them Mavis and Myrtle – are about to start their weekly round of golf. Mavis suggests they make it a little

* www.tonyrobbins.com/ask-tony/power-of-compounding/

more interesting this week by putting a wager on each hole. It'll just be a small wager, something to add a bit of spice to the game. Mavis suggests the loser pays the winner of each hole 10 cents, and that the wager doubles when they move on to the next hole.

"Okay, 10 cents? What could I lose?" thinks Myrtle and readily accepts. There's only 18 holes, so 10 cents a hole is $1.80, and that doubled makes it $3.60. Not even enough for a shandy at the 19th hole. But is it?

Let's look at what happens in the first six holes:

| | |
|---|---:|
| Hole 1 | $0.10 |
| Hole 2 | $0.20 |
| Hole 3 | $0.40 |
| Hole 4 | $0.80 |
| Hole 5 | $1.60 |
| Hole 6 | $3.20 |

Okay, well that's a little more than what Myrtle was expecting, but still, we are a third of the way through the course, and the balance we are up to is $3.20 per hole. What's the worst that could happen? Maybe the last hole will cost $20 to $30?

| | |
|---|---:|
| Hole 7 | $6.40 |
| Hole 8 | $12.80 |
| Hole 9 | $25.60 |

Whoa, in three holes, we went from $3.20 a hole to $25.60 a hole. Myrtle has the same look in her eye as that time when her husband (a retired accountant) announced he was going to renovate the bathroom by himself.

| Hole 10 | $51.20 |
|---|---|
| Hole 11 | $102.40 |
| Hole 12 | $204.80 |
| Hole 13 | $409.60 |
| Hole 14 | $819.20 |

Myrtle is shitting bricks.

| Hole 15 | $1,638.40 |
|---|---|

Myrtle feigns a ligament injury to her shoulder and promptly heads for the car. Lucky, because check out what goes down on the last three holes.

| Hole 16 | $3,276.80 |
|---|---|
| Hole 17 | $6,553.60 |
| Hole 18 | $13,107.20 |

The moral of the story? Well, a lot of people will tell you that this is an example of compound growth, but really, it is exponential growth. And it's a really aggressive example. Doubling your money at each step is the same as 100% growth. There's no way we can relate that to home loans, right?

Well, maybe.

Banks would love us to think that the interest rate is the be-all and end-all when it comes to home loans. Most people believe that in the golf analogy above, it is the interest rate (100%) that is the most important factor. In reality, though, it is not the interest rate alone that creates the massive growth from 10 cents to over $13,000; it is also the number of times the interest is calculated.

If it was only calculated once, the 10 cents would only grow to 20 cents. But the more times the calculation is repeated, the larger the figure becomes.

It is the same with home loans. The initial balance of the loan and the interest rate might appear to be low or at least manageable. But if the bank is adding interest to the loan every single month for 30 years, that's 360 repetitions.

The longer it takes you to pay off the loan, the more money the bank makes. All due to the most powerful force in the universe according to Albert Einstein – compound interest. (He never said this, but why let that ruin a good story?)

Put simply, compound interest is where interest is calculated on interest. When you have savings in the bank, this works in your favour. The interest you earned in the first month of your term deposit is added to the balance, and therefore, in the second month, you are earning interest on the interest that you earned in the first month.

And it should come as no surprise that if the banks offer us products such as term deposits and high-interest savings accounts on which we can earn interest on our interest, they also have a few products that do the same for them. The difference? Theirs are on steroids.

## SUMMARY

Knowing how interest on your home loan is calculated is vitally important. It is the basis of ALL the home loan hacks.

Interest is quoted annually, charged monthly, and most importantly – calculated daily.

How much interest you pay in a month is determined by your loan balance, the interest rate, and how many days are in that month.

When the interest from the first month is added to your loan, the bank will then be charging you interest on that interest in the second month. In the third month, you are paying interest on the interest on the interest.

PART 3

# THE HACKS

## IN THIS SECTION, YOU WILL LEARN:

The basic hacks that can save a stack of interest.

How combining them can save you even more.

How changing your cash flow can work in your favour.

That redraw and offset are two very different things.

## CHAPTER SEVEN

# The Kindy-Level Debt-Reduction Tips from the Bank

Okay, so now you know The Bad and Ugly aspects of home loans, it is time to apply some hacks to get to The Good.

You've gone to the bank and asked them what you can do to pay off your loan faster.

Before we delve too deep here, let's just reflect on this scene. We are asking the bank for advice on how to reduce our debt. This, in turn, will reduce the amount of interest they earn. It's just like going into a greasy fish and chips shop and asking them for a diet plan. So, just keep in mind when we ask the bank how we can reduce our debt faster, their answer may, in fact, still be all about them.

The two strategies that you are most likely to hear are:

- Pay more regularly than monthly.
- Pay more than the minimum amount required.

Good strategies. Basic. But good.

## Paying More Regularly

**HACK #1**

*Pay more regularly (than monthly).*

Here's a graph that shows how a loan term can be reduced simply by changing the repayment frequency from monthly to fortnightly.

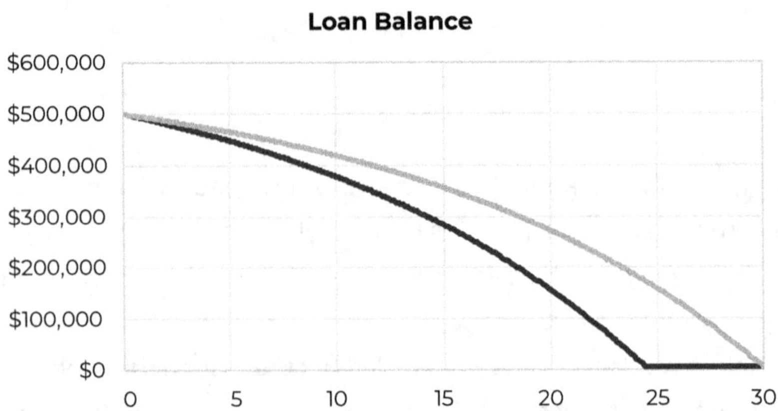


Paying fortnightly automatically reduces the loan term from 30 years to 25 years and will save you $128,180 in interest by doing so. How simple is this hack? Just ring the bank and tell them to change your repayment to fortnightly, and, hey presto, you're debt-free five years sooner and $128k richer.

| Repayment Comparison | Monthly | Fortnightly |
|---|---|---|
| Min. Repayment | $2,998 | $1,499 |
| Loan Payoff Terms | 30.00 | 24.39 |
| Payoff Years Saved | | 5.6 |
| Total Interest & Fee Paid | $579,985 | $451,805 |
| Total Interest & Fee Saved | | $128,180 |

### Is Weekly Better?

Yes and no. If we do the comparison calculation on the above figures and compare paying monthly, fortnightly, and weekly, weekly comes out on top – by a whopping $546 over 30 years. Yep, paying fortnightly will save you $128,180, and paying weekly will save you $128,726.

Woo-hooo, we are eating lobster tonight, baby.

| Repayment Comparison | Monthly | Fortnightly | Weekly |
|---|---|---|---|
| Min. Repayment | $2,998 | $1,499 | $749 |
| Loan Payoff Terms | 30.00 | 24.39 | 24.36 |
| Payoff Years Saved | | 5.6 | 5.6 |
| Total Interest & Fee Paid | $579,985 | $451,805 | $451,258 |
| Total Interest & Fee Saved | | $128,180 | $128,726 |

So how does this work? Why does just changing the repayment frequency have such a significant effect? Two reasons:

1. The fortnightly or weekly repayment is higher than it should be.

   There's a big difference between a true fortnightly repayment and an accelerated fortnightly repayment. There are 26 fortnights and 52 weeks per year. A true fortnightly repayment is calculated by multiplying the monthly repayment by 12 to get an annual figure, then dividing this by 26 to get the fortnightly figure. If this is how your bank calculates the fortnightly repayment, then there is very little difference between this and paying monthly.

An accelerated fortnightly repayment is simply the monthly repayment divided by 2. But we know there are more than two fortnights in a month, so by making a half-monthly payment 26 times a year, we've actually paid 13 months' worth of repayments in 12 months. You are paying more than the minimum, and this is naturally going to reduce your loan faster than if you had made the minimum monthly repayment.

2. By paying more regularly, you are reducing the balance of the loan that interest is calculated on sooner than if you were paying monthly. This will reduce the daily interest calculation.

Let's go back to our daily interest table and compare it to the same month but with accelerated fortnightly repayments.

Loan Balance: $500,000
Interest Rate: 6%

A minimum monthly repayment gets paid at the end of the month, so the balance does not change for the whole month.

An accelerated fortnightly repayment is made on 18 January and 1 February, meaning the loan balance that daily interest is calculated on immediately reduces after these payments.

| | Minimum Monthly Repayment | | Accelerated Fortnightly Repayment | | |
|---|---|---|---|---|---|
| Date | Loan Balance | Daily Interest | | Loan Balance | Daily Interest |
| 15 January | $500,000 | $82.19 | | $500,000 | $82.19 |
| 16 January | $500,000 | $82.19 | | $500,000 | $82.19 |
| 17 January | $500,000 | $82.19 | | $500,000 | $82.19 |
| 18 January | $500,000 | $82.19 | $1,499 Payment | $498,501 | $81.94 |
| 19 January | $500,000 | $82.19 | | $498,501 | $81.94 |
| 20 January | $500,000 | $82.19 | | $498,501 | $81.94 |
| 21 January | $500,000 | $82.19 | | $498,501 | $81.94 |
| 22 January | $500,000 | $82.19 | | $498,501 | $81.94 |
| 23 January | $500,000 | $82.19 | | $498,501 | $81.94 |
| 24 January | $500,000 | $82.19 | | $498,501 | $81.94 |
| 25 January | $500,000 | $82.19 | | $498,501 | $81.94 |
| 26 January | $500,000 | $82.19 | | $498,501 | $81.94 |
| 27 January | $500,000 | $82.19 | | $498,501 | $81.94 |
| 28 January | $500,000 | $82.19 | | $498,501 | $81.94 |
| 29 January | $500,000 | $82.19 | | $498,501 | $81.94 |
| 30 January | $500,000 | $82.19 | | $498,501 | $81.94 |
| 31 January | $500,000 | $82.19 | | $498,501 | $81.94 |
| 01 February | $500,000 | $82.19 | $1,499 Payment | $497,002 | $81.70 |
| 02 February | $500,000 | $82.19 | | $497,002 | $81.70 |
| 03 February | $500,000 | $82.19 | | $497,002 | $81.70 |
| 04 February | $500,000 | $82.19 | | $497,002 | $81.70 |
| 05 February | $500,000 | $82.19 | | $497,002 | $81.70 |
| 06 February | $500,000 | $82.19 | | $497,002 | $81.70 |
| 07 February | $500,000 | $82.19 | | $497,002 | $81.70 |
| 08 February | $500,000 | $82.19 | | $497,002 | $81.70 |
| 09 February | $500,000 | $82.19 | | $497,002 | $81.70 |
| 10 February | $500,000 | $82.19 | | $497,002 | $81.70 |

| | Minimum Monthly Repayment | | Accelerated Fortnightly Repayment | | |
|---|---|---|---|---|---|
| Date | Loan Balance | Daily Interest | | Loan Balance | Daily Interest |
| 11 February | $500,000 | $82.19 | | $497,002 | $81.70 |
| 12 February | $500,000 | $82.19 | | $497,002 | $81.70 |
| 13 February | $500,000 | $82.19 | | $497,002 | $81.70 |
| 14 February | $500,000 | $82.19 | | $497,002 | $81.70 |
| | | **$2,547.89** | | | **$2,537.53** |

As you can see, instead of keeping your balance at the highest possible amount of $500,000 for the whole month, by paying fortnightly, you have reduced the balance the interest is calculated on. This, in turn, has saved you just over $10 in interest payable to the bank for that month, and while $10 doesn't seem like much, repeat it every single month for 30 years, and see what happens. Myrtle would see the value.

### *Book Recommendation* – The Slight Edge *by Jeff Olson*

Do yourself a favour and grab this book. Paperback, Kindle, Audible – it doesn't matter.

Jeff Olson explains how small actions repeated many times over long periods can result in monumental change. These actions are usually really easy to do, but most importantly, they are also easy NOT to do. For example, exercise. For most people, it is pretty easy to go for a 30minute walk each day. If you walk for 30 minutes every day, then in most cases, your health will improve. But it is really easy to wake up one morning, see a few clouds, and decide against the walk in favour of another hour in bed.

That then makes it even easier to skip another walk later in the week when you've got a busy day ahead of you. In fact, the excuses you make for not going for a walk every single day become easier and easier to justify. Before you know it, you are barely going for a single walk each week.

And who is going to be healthier? The you who walks every single morning regardless of the weather, or the you who makes the easy decision to miss a few days? Peer into that crystal ball and have a look at these different versions of you five years into the future. Who is going to have the firmer glutes, increased lung capacity, and decreased risk of a variety of diseases?

It's the same with money. That $3 in interest you save by simply changing the repayment frequency from monthly to fortnightly is really easy to set up. It's also really easy to not set up, especially when you think it's a trivial amount. But $3 saved every month over many years adds up to become a significant amount of money, especially if it is compounding in your favour.

Okay, back to our exciting calculations. No, I didn't misspell "long-winded".

This is a good result, right? By paying fortnightly, you have reduced the amount of interest you paid that month by $10. But is it? Could you have saved more?

### Aligning Your Repayment with Your Income

Even though the savings compared to paying fortnightly are not great, I'm still a big fan of making your mortgage repayments weekly. But here's the caveat – only if you get paid weekly.

In most cases, home loan borrowers achieve the greatest

efficiency when they align their mortgage repayments with their income. If they get paid monthly, then they make their repayment monthly. If they get paid fortnightly, pay the home loan fortnightly. Get paid weekly? Repay weekly.

Why? Two reasons.

The first is that you can't spend money that you don't have. As your wages come in, making your home loan repayment soon after will ensure that this important bill is always paid. Leave it in there for a week before the repayment is due, and there's a chance you've gone silly at the bait and tackle shop in the interim, and you might now be a bit short when the payment is due. Aligning your wages and home loan repayments avoids this risk.

The second reason is best demonstrated by the table comparing the monthly and fortnightly payments above, which shows that the sooner you can reduce the balance of the loan, the less daily interest you will pay.

### What If I Get Paid Monthly?

If you get paid monthly, then there is very little benefit in paying fortnightly or weekly. This is something I see very often – people who get paid monthly but pay their mortgage fortnightly because they have heard this will help reduce their debt faster.

Let's say you get paid monthly on the 16th of each month. Your hard-earned wages hit your savings account on the 16th, and your fortnightly repayment comes out the next day, on the 17th, and then again 14 days later. Here's what our example month looks like:

Remember that a few pages back we looked at what the monthly interest would be if you had kept your balance at $500,000 for the whole month. That amount was $2,547.89.

| Date | Loan Day of the Month | Loan Balance | Annual Interest Rate | Daily Interest |
|---|---|---|---|---|
| 15 January | 1 | $500,000 | 6% | $82.19 |
| 16 January | 2 | $500,000 | 6% | $82.19 |
| | Payday. Monthly wages deposited into your savings account | | | |
| 17 January | 3 | $500,000 | 6% | $82.19 |
| 18 January | Fortnightly Repayment Day. $1,499 transferred to home loan. | | | |
| | 4 | $498,501 | 6% | $81.94 |
| 19 January | 5 | $498,501 | 6% | $81.94 |
| 20 January | 6 | $498,501 | 6% | $81.94 |
| 21 January | 7 | $498,501 | 6% | $81.94 |
| 22 January | 8 | $498,501 | 6% | $81.94 |
| 23 January | 9 | $498,501 | 6% | $81.94 |
| 24 January | 10 | $498,501 | 6% | $81.94 |
| 25 January | 11 | $498,501 | 6% | $81.94 |
| 26 January | 12 | $498,501 | 6% | $81.94 |
| 27 January | 13 | $498,501 | 6% | $81.94 |
| 28 January | 14 | $498,501 | 6% | $81.94 |
| 29 January | 15 | $498,501 | 6% | $81.94 |
| 30 January | 16 | $498,501 | 6% | $81.94 |
| 31 January | 17 | $498,501 | 6% | $81.94 |
| 01 February | Fortnightly Repayment Day. $1,499 transferred to home loan. | | | |
| | 18 | $497,002 | 6% | $81.70 |
| 02 February | 19 | $497,002 | 6% | $81.70 |
| 03 February | 20 | $497,002 | 6% | $81.70 |
| 04 February | 21 | $497,002 | 6% | $81.70 |
| 05 February | 22 | $497,002 | 6% | $81.70 |
| 06 February | 23 | $497,002 | 6% | $81.70 |

| Date | Loan Day of the Month | Loan Balance | Annual Interest Rate | Daily Interest |
|---|---|---|---|---|
| 07 February | 24 | $497,002 | 6% | $81.70 |
| 08 February | 25 | $497,002 | 6% | $81.70 |
| 09 February | 26 | $497,002 | 6% | $81.70 |
| 10 February | 27 | $497,002 | 6% | $81.70 |
| 11 February | 28 | $497,002 | 6% | $81.70 |
| 12 February | 29 | $497,002 | 6% | $81.70 |
| 13 February | 30 | $497,002 | 6% | $81.70 |
| 14 February | 31 | $497,002 | 6% | $81.70 |
| | | | **Total** | **$2,537.53** |

In the above example, you received your monthly pay on the 16th and then made a fortnightly repayment on the 18th and another one on the first of the next month. This means that you had to make sure that you had at least $1,499 in your savings account at all times to ensure that your next fortnightly payment was able to be made. If it is sitting in your savings account earning nothing, instead of making two smaller fortnightly repayments, why not just make one larger monthly payment on the 16th?

| Date | Loan Day of the Month | Loan Balance | Annual Interest Rate | Daily Interest |
|---|---|---|---|---|
| 15 January | 1 | $500,000 | 6% | $82.19 |
| 16 January | 2 | $500,000 | 6% | $82.19 |
| | Payday. Monthly wages deposited into your savings account | | | |
| 17 January | 3 | $500,000 | 6% | $82.19 |
| 18 January | Monthly Repayment Day. $2,998 transferred to home loan. | | | |
| | 4 | $497,002 | 6% | $81.70 |

| Date | Loan Day of the Month | Loan Balance | Annual Interest Rate | Daily Interest |
|---|---|---|---|---|
| 19 January | 5 | $497,002 | 6% | $81.70 |
| 20 January | 6 | $497,002 | 6% | $81.70 |
| 21 January | 7 | $497,002 | 6% | $81.70 |
| 22 January | 8 | $497,002 | 6% | $81.70 |
| 23 January | 9 | $497,002 | 6% | $81.70 |
| 24 January | 10 | $497,002 | 6% | $81.70 |
| 25 January | 11 | $497,002 | 6% | $81.70 |
| 26 January | 12 | $497,002 | 6% | $81.70 |
| 27 January | 13 | $497,002 | 6% | $81.70 |
| 28 January | 14 | $497,002 | 6% | $81.70 |
| 29 January | 15 | $497,002 | 6% | $81.70 |
| 30 January | 16 | $497,002 | 6% | $81.70 |
| 31 January | 17 | $497,002 | 6% | $81.70 |
| 01 February | 18 | $497,002 | 6% | $81.70 |
| 02 February | 19 | $497,002 | 6% | $81.70 |
| 03 February | 20 | $497,002 | 6% | $81.70 |
| 04 February | 21 | $497,002 | 6% | $81.70 |
| 05 February | 22 | $497,002 | 6% | $81.70 |
| 06 February | 23 | $497,002 | 6% | $81.70 |
| 07 February | 24 | $497,002 | 6% | $81.70 |
| 08 February | 25 | $497,002 | 6% | $81.70 |
| 09 February | 26 | $497,002 | 6% | $81.70 |
| 10 February | 27 | $497,002 | 6% | $81.70 |
| 11 February | 28 | $497,002 | 6% | $81.70 |
| 12 February | 29 | $497,002 | 6% | $81.70 |
| 13 February | 30 | $497,002 | 6% | $81.70 |
| 14 February | 31 | $497,002 | 6% | $81.70 |
| | | | **Total** | **$2,534.17** |

Yay, you've saved another $3.

There's a psychological benefit of doing this as well. Keeping an eye on your savings balance throughout the month to ensure you have enough to make the next fortnightly repayment can be stressful. Making a large monthly payment soon after you get your monthly income means the loan is looked after until after your next payday, and you can't be tempted to spend what you don't have.

This may all seem trivial, but what I'm trying to get across here is the importance of knowing how interest is calculated, and especially knowing that it is calculated daily.

This means the daily balance of the loan is all-important. Reduce the daily balance of the loan by as much as you can as early as you can, and this will reduce the amount of interest that you pay.

Paying more regularly than monthly is one way of doing it, but it's most effective when you align your repayments to your income frequency.

Next time you speak to a bank staff, ask them whether they recommend you pay your mortgage monthly or fortnightly. Then ask them if your income frequency matters at all. Those who know how daily interest is calculated should give you an honest answer that confirms my suggestions, but a stack of them won't.

The results? On a $500k loan, and assuming fortnightly income, changing the loan repayments from the minimum monthly to the minimum fortnightly amount will shave five years and six months off the term of the loan and in that time save $128,180 worth of interest. Pretty sweet returns for just aligning your repayments to your income.

## Paying More than the Minimum

**HACK #2**

*Pay more than the minimum.*

This is the other old chestnut that the banks love to trot out. And don't get me wrong – it is great advice. But if this is the limit of their advice on how you can reduce your debt faster, then you know you're dealing with amateurs.

Paying more than the minimum repayment reduces your debt faster than if you just make the minimum repayment. Wow, did I really just write that? I know it sounds ridiculously obvious, but you'd be surprised by the number of people who have never even considered doing this.

It works in a two-fold way. First, you are reducing the balance by more than the minimum required to retire the debt in 30 years. This is naturally going to mean that you will be debt-free in less than 30 years.

Secondly, as soon as you make that extra repayment, the balance of the loan is immediately reduced, and now the bank can only calculate daily interest on that lower amount. This, in turn, means you pay less interest. As you are still making your standard repayment, if less of that amount is interest, then as a result, more of it is principal.

So, not only have you made a small lump sum payment on the loan, just by doing that, you have decreased the amount of interest you pay and increased the amount of principal coming off your next payment. So simple, but powerful in a three-pronged way.

1. Reduces the balance of the loan.
2. Reduces the amount of interest you pay in your next payment.
3. Increases the amount of principal you pay in your next payment.

I know what you're thinking. Enough with the words, Hirsty. Show me some maths.

Let's take our $500k loan and add just $100 a month to the repayment. I know for some of you that is going to be extremely difficult. For others, it will be merely forgoing the entrée during one of the many long lunches taken with colleagues at the Michelin 3-star restaurant overlooking the harbour.

Some of you will be able to make extra repayments, and some of you won't. The purpose of this calculation is just to show the effects such an extra repayment can have.

A $100 extra repayment per month will pay off the loan 2.5 years early and will save $57,744 in interest over that time.

| Repayment Comparison | Minimum Monthly | Extra $100 |
|---|---|---|
| Min. Repayment | $2,998 | $2,998 |
| Max. Extra Repayment | | $100 |
| Loan Paid Off (Years) | 30.00 | 27.50 |
| Years Saved | | 2.5 |
| Total Interest Paid | $579,985 | $522,240 |
| **Total Interest Saved** | | **$57,744** |

What if you could spare $1,000 per month?

| Repayment Comparison | Minimum Monthly | Extra $1,000 |
|---|---|---|
| Min. Repayment | $2,998 | $2,998 |
| Max. Extra Repayment | | $1,000 |
| Loan Paid Off (Years) | 30.00 | 16.42 |
| Years Saved | | 13.6 |
| Total Interest Paid | $579,985 | $287,076 |
| **Total Interest Saved** | | **$292,909** |

CHAPTER EIGHT

# More than the Minimum, More Regularly

Now you know the two basic, kindergarten-level debt-reduction tips from the bank.

**Hack #1 –** Pay more regularly (but make sure this aligns with your income frequency).

**Hack #2 –** Pay more than the minimum.

Just for fun, let's combine them.

**HACK #3**

*Pay more than the minimum, more regularly.*

Let's halve those extra monthly amounts and set the repayments to fortnightly:

| Repayment Comparison | Minimum Monthly | Minimum Fortnightly | Extra $50 Fortnightly |
|---|---|---|---|
| Min. Repayment | $2,998 | $1,499 | $1,499 |
| Extra Repayment | | $0 | $50 |
| Loan Paid Off (Years) | 30.00 | 24.39 | 22.67 |
| Years Saved | | 5.6 | 7.3 |
| Total Interest Paid | $579,985 | $451,805 | $415,255 |
| **Total Interest Saved** | | **$128,180** | **$164,730** |

By now, I'm really hoping that the maths is well and truly sinking in. I know for a lot of you this is basic stuff that you already know, and I'm certainly not trying to belittle you by explaining it. I want to start at the basics and move to more complex calculations, and the explanations above are designed to ensure that everyone can get their head around how interest is calculated.

## Key Points

Interest is calculated daily.

The sooner you reduce the balance of the loan, the less interest you will pay.

## The Traditional Cash Flow

The more you can reduce the loan amount by, the less interest you will pay.

You might think that the banks make their money through charging interest and fees, and you'd be totally right. But what actually allows them to do this? It's because they usually set up your loan accounts and cash flow in a way that allows them to charge the highest possible daily interest every single day.

The banks have been very successful in training all of us on how a standard cash flow is structured. Ever since we were about a metre tall and taking our 50-cent piece to school with our school banking account book, we've been led to believe that the only way of moving our money around is precisely the way that makes them the most amount of money. What a coincidence.

The typical Australian cash flow follows these basic steps:

- Income is deposited into a "savings" account (this could also be called a "cheque" account).
- All loan repayments and expenditure are taken from this "savings account".

Yes, the quotation marks are deliberate. I mean, seriously, what the hell is a "cheque"? And these are not "savings" accounts – they are "spending" accounts. The banks don't want us to save this money; they want us to spend it.

If they really wanted us to save this money, they would call our balance "savings" on their internet banking platforms and ATM receipts, but instead they call it our "available balance" – just a subtle reminder that our job is to take advantage of what is available.

Here's a diagram of a typical Australian cash flow:

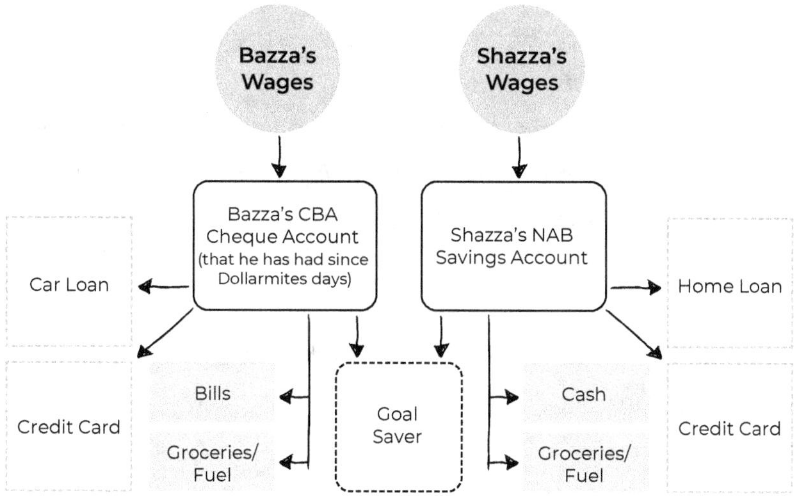


This cash flow makes sense to Bazza and Shazza, and this is how they justify it.

Their income goes into separate individual spending accounts.

Bazza: *We've always had separate bank accounts that our income goes into. It's just what we've always done.*

Shazza: *It's nice to have a bit of privacy with our spending. I love Baz, but he tends to whinge a bit when he finds out how much it costs a woman to go to the hairdresser these days. It's easy to be judgemental when you are bald. Having my own account helps keep us a happy couple.*

They separate responsibility for payment of their debts. Shazza pays the mortgage while Bazza pays the car loan.

Shazza: *I earn more, so I pay the home loan.*

Bazza: *Shaz isn't interested in cars, so the car is mine, and I look after that loan.*

Dave: *Shazza, do you know what the balance of the car loan is, and what the interest rate and repayments are?*

Shazza: ...

They deposit a little income each fortnight into a joint high-interest savings account.

Shazza: *We are saving for a holiday to Hawaii, and we put any extra money into the Goal Saver account as we earn high interest on this. It's just a savings account, so we don't have an ATM card for it.*

They have a credit card each.

Bazza: *I don't use mine. It's just for emergencies.* (Translation: It is maxed out.)

Shazza: *I just have it for online purchases and bookings – things you can't use a debit card for.* (Translation: It is maxed out.)

They take cash out each week.

Bazza: *You have to have some cash on you. Coffees, lunches, my shout at the pub.*

Shazza: *I go to the markets on the weekends, and most of the traders only accept cash.*

Let's leave Bazza and Shazza for a moment and look at your cash flow. What does it look like? Try mapping it out using these shapes and colours.

**Green Circles: Income.** Break all your sources of income up, so have one circle for your wages, one for your rental income, one for Centrelink, etc.

**Blue Squares: Savings/cheque accounts.** List your day-to-day accounts as well as any kids' accounts, term deposits, and high-interest savings accounts.

**Red Squares: Debt.** Include your home loan, personal loan, car loan, credit card, Buy Now, Pay Later, etc.

**Orange Rectangles: Expenditure items.** You could go crazy here and list all the different things you spend money on, but first of all, maybe just look at your major groups, such as bills, groceries, fuel, and general living.

Join them all together with arrows so you can see the direction of the cash flow.

Now that's done, what does it look like? Is it a bit of a dog's breakfast? Like Bazza and Shazza, are you running multiple spending accounts and have money moving around like flies on a picnic? If so, when was the last time you got a Christmas card from your bank, because you are basically gift wrapping your cash flow and handing it to your bank and asking them to screw you over in the best way possible.

Here's how the bank looks at this cash flow.

Bazza and Shazza's income goes into separate individual spending accounts.

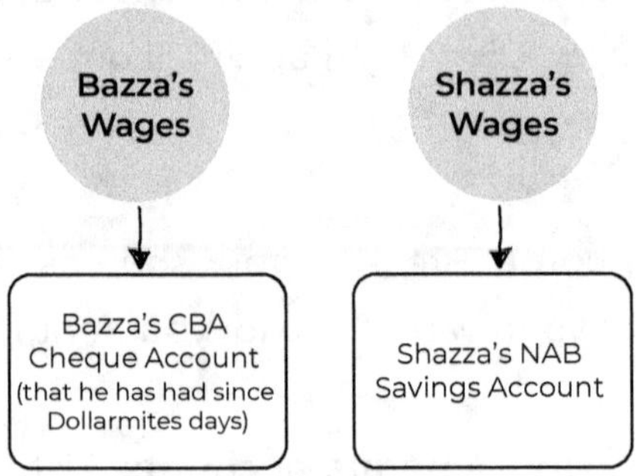


Bank: *Perfect – just like we taught them in primary school. Run separate accounts so they are only accountable for their own spending. People tend to spend less when they know their partner will also see their transactions.*

They separate responsibility for payment of their debts.

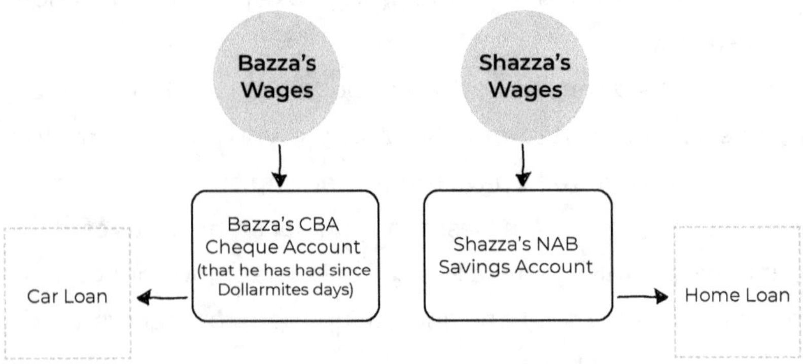


Bank: *Ah, diluting responsibility again. Knowledge is power, and when you don't know what's going on with all your debts, you don't have any power.*

They deposit a little income each fortnight into a joint high-interest savings account.

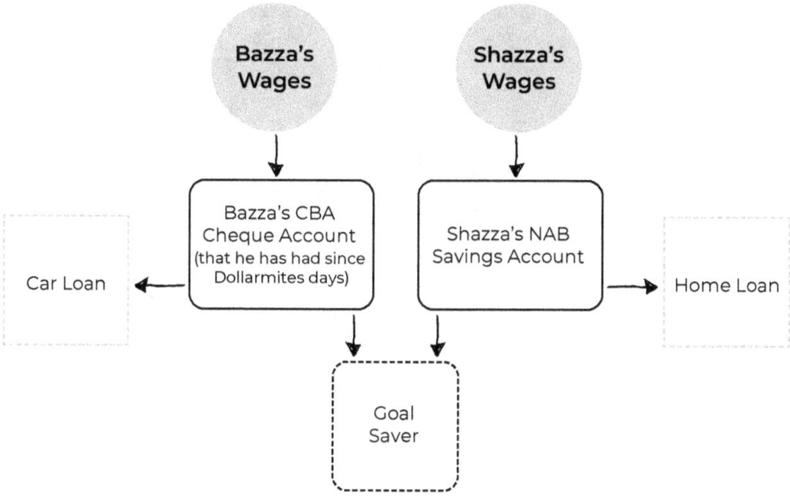


Bank: *One of the greatest cons around. We trick people into believing that they are earning stacks of interest on their "high-interest" savings account, when in reality, it is about half the home loan rate. The client then also has to pay tax on the interest they earn, so this reduces the effective rate by another 30% or so, and then inflation kills whatever remaining benefit there is for the client.*

They have a credit card each.

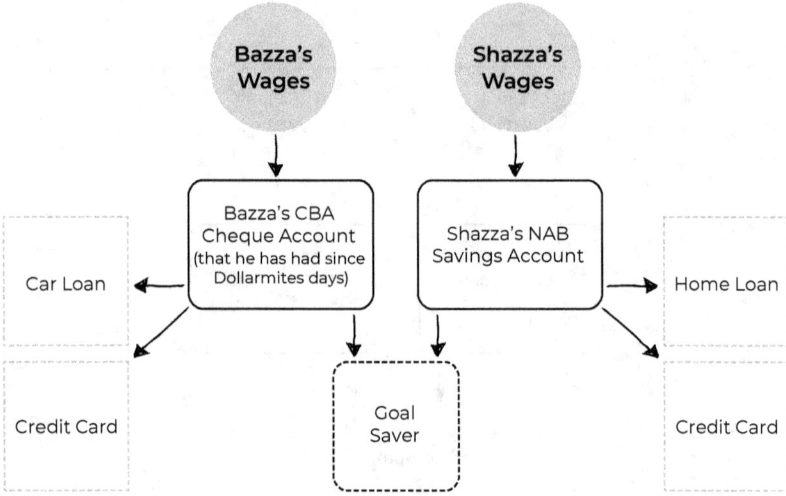


Bank: *Double the annual fees and double the interest. Hopefully they are both late with their payment each month so we can sting them two late payment and over-limit fees as well.*

They take cash out each week.

Bank: *If their money is sitting in their wallet, then we don't have to pay any interest on it (as meagre as that would be). Cash in your pocket doesn't earn interest, and it doesn't save interest, so this is the best-case scenario for us bankers.*

To summarise, Baz and Shaz are moving their money around in a way that the bank loves. They have several accounts, loans, and credit cards, and this makes it all but impossible to track effectively. It also means that the more accounts they have, the more fees they are being charged. But most importantly, this structure allows the bank to pay the minimum amount of interest on savings and charge the maximum amount of interest on the loans.

## Earning Interest vs Saving Interest

Sorry to tell you, if you have debts and are also trying to save money, then you're doing it all wrong. Saving interest, rather than earning interest, is where the party is at.

I'm going to go easy on Shaz and Baz for a bit and make this really simple. Let's say you have a home loan and a high-interest savings account. Let's also assume you have received a windfall of $10,000 and want to know where you should park it for the best return.

You will never find a high-interest savings account that offers you a similar or higher interest rate than the home loan. If the home loan rate is 6%, then you'd be lucky to get a high-interest account paying you 4%, so let's work on these figures.

You park your $10,000 in the savings account, and you start earning daily interest on that from the moment it is deposited. After a month, you've earned an astonishing $33.

$$\$10{,}000 \times 4\% \div 12$$

That's pretty sweet – $33 in my account without really doing anything. There's a catch, right?

Yep. Tax.

**Rule #1 – You pay tax on interest that you earn.**

You get taxed on any and all income that you earn (or declare for those naughty so-and-sos amongst you). If his annual salary is $75,000, his marginal tax rate is 30%, and this means that of the $33 that Baz earned in interest, he has to pay $9.90 of it to the tax office.

In reality, his high-interest savings account has paid him an after-tax income of $23.10.

We can reverse calculate that to show that even though the bank is advertising the interest rate as 4%, he is actually only getting 2.77% after tax.

> ***Clarification*** – Tax on your savings is not typically collected every month. It all gets worked out at the end of the year when your tax return is lodged. I'm just using monthly figures here so we can compare it to our home loan scenario.

**Rule #2 – You DON'T pay tax on interest that you save.**

If Baz deposited the $10k into his home loan, he immediately reduces the balance that interest is calculated on by – you guessed it – $10k. So now his home loan balance is $490,000 instead of $500,000. He won't be earning any interest on that, but he will be saving the home loan interest rate on it.

By depositing $10,000 into his 6% home loan, Baz will reduce his monthly interest calculation by $50.

$10,000 × 6% = $600 per year.

$600 ÷ 12 months = $50

And here's the kicker – our fearless leaders in Canberra won't get a cent of it. You see, they cannot tax us on interest that we save, so this $50 is all for Baz. This is $26.90 better return per month compared to the high-interest savings account.

To get a similar return after tax on the savings account, the interest rate he would need to earn would be 7.8%.

Moral of the story? Saving interest is often more powerful than earning it.

Back to Baz and Shaz's cash flow.

I know it is very subtle, but see if you can work out from the diagram below where they are keeping their money in accounts that give them the worst return.

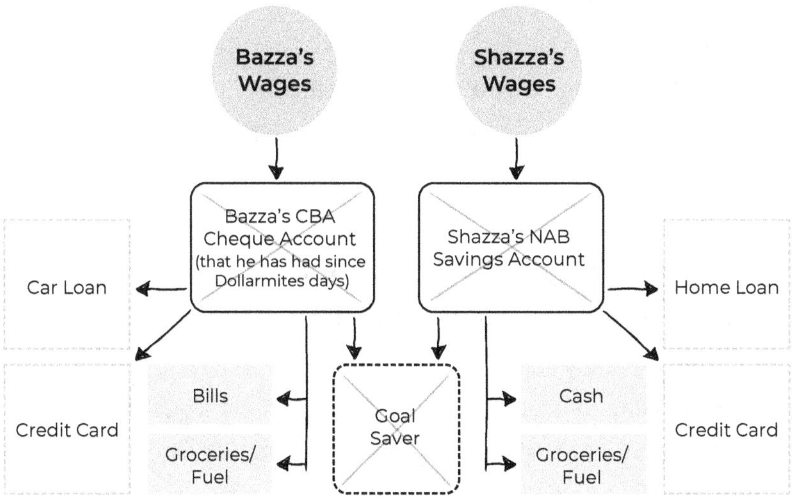

### *Debt Consolidation*

Once you've mapped out your cash flow and accounts, the next step is to identify the ones that are costing you the most and aim to get rid of them. If the heroes of our story want to become debt-free as quickly as possible, then it would be a lot easier if they had just the single debt to focus on. But increasing the home loan to pay out the credit cards and car loan is not always the best idea. You could be turning a five-year car loan into a 30-year car loan if you consolidate it into the home loan.

### *Know Your Problem*

Do you have a debt problem or a spending problem? If you have a spending problem, then the only thing that debt consolidation will do is allow you to spend even more. The result is more debt and another maxed-out credit card that your bank will be all too happy to suggest you again consolidate into the home loan, starting the process off again.

## Parking Your Pay in Your Home Loan

By now, you know two things for sure:

1. Banks calculate interest on your home loan DAILY.
2. The less you owe on any given day, the less interest they can charge you.

So, here's a radical idea: instead of letting your pay sit idle in a savings account, why not throw it straight at your home loan the minute it is paid?

Yep, we're going to park your pay in your loan.

Not forever. Just until you need it.

Let's break this down.

## HACK #4

***Get your income paid directly into the home loan.***

Most Australians get paid into a transaction or savings account. From there, they drip-feed money out for groceries, bills, Friday-night takeaway, multiple streaming subscriptions. Meanwhile, their home loan balance is sitting there at full strength, racking up the maximum possible daily interest.

Now imagine instead that your pay goes into the home loan itself. Every dollar temporarily reduces your loan balance, even if it's just for a few days. You save interest immediately. You can still pull it back out as needed, assuming your loan has what's called "free redraw".

That's the hack.

Almost all variable rate home loans allow you to make extra repayments above your required monthly amount. Redraw means you can then access that money again later. It's like having a savings account inside your loan.

Here's how it works:

- Jim gets paid $5,000.
- He gets his employer to deposit it straight into his home loan.
- His balance goes from $500,000 to $495,000.

- Daily interest is now calculated on $495,000.
- Over the next 2–3 weeks, Jim draws funds back out to cover his expenses.

Even if Jim only leaves the money in for a few days, he's still ahead.

Every day his balance is lower than normal = interest saved.

## Jim vs Bazza – The Showdown

Let's say Bazza parks his $5,000 pay in a savings account paying 4% interest. Over a month, he earns about $11.67 in interest after tax.

Jim parks his $5,000 in his home loan with a 6% interest rate. He saves about $25 in interest that month.

And here's the kicker: the $25 Jim saves isn't taxed.

Jim: 1. Bazza: 0.

The catch? How will Jim pay for his weekly Aldi shop?

What he will need is redraw – the ability to get that extra $5k payment back out again when he has expenses.

Directing your salary into the loan only works if:

- Your loan allows free unlimited redraws.
- The redraw process is fast (preferably instant).
- You're disciplined enough not to panic just because your transaction account balance says $0.

Some lenders charge fees or have delays when moving money in and out. If that's the case, you might not want to throw all your income into the loan. You could leave a float (say $500–$1000) in a regular account for peace of mind.

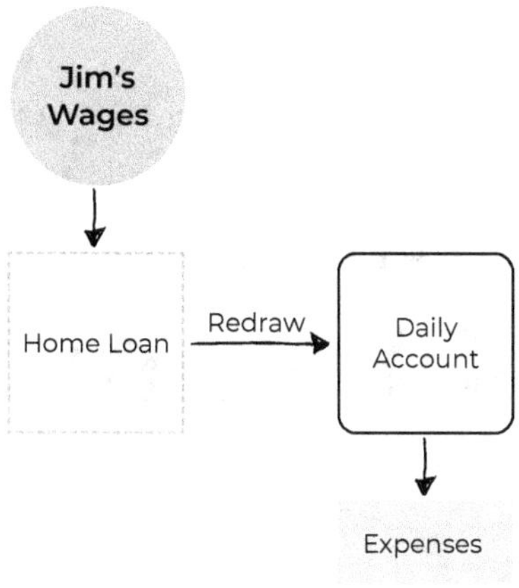


If Jim gets a $5,000 salary deposit, it goes straight into the home loan and reduces the balance of the loan to $495k. Now the bank can only calculate daily interest on $495k instead of $500k.

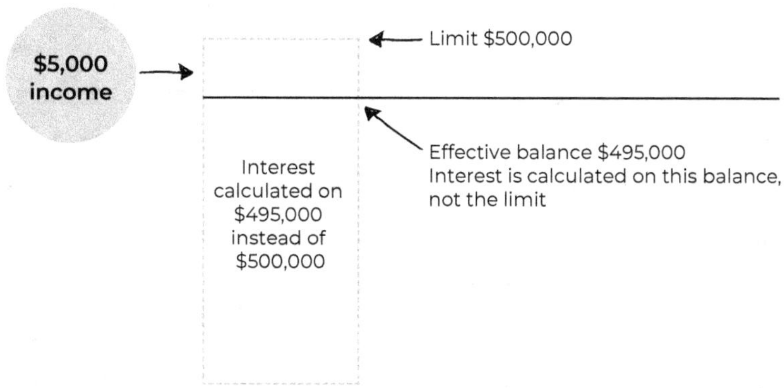

## CHAPTER NINE

# The All-In-One Loan

### The now-extinct Line of Credit

Don't get too excited about the next option, as it really doesn't exist anymore. Well, that's not entirely true. Some banks still offer them but the interest rates are eye-watering. So why am I even including it? Truth be told, it was a really good loan product that made sense and allowed a lot of people to pay off their loan sooner. Maybe that's why the banks got rid of them.

Once upon a time, there was a magical beast called the "line of credit loan". Think of it like a home loan crossed with a transaction account. Every deposit reduced your loan balance. Every expense increased it.

With this setup, your home loan was also your transaction account. Income was deposited directly into it, which immediately reduced the balance that interest was calculated on.

When you had to pay a bill, you paid it directly out of the home loan itself. The home loan came with a debit card as well, so you could do your shopping and fill the car up at the servo and pay for it with the available funds in your home loan.

This pushed the balance up, and therefore the daily interest calculation went up with it.

Sounds simple, right? If you had to imagine the most flexible loan product that allowed you to reduce the balance that interest was calculated on, you'd probably come up with the line of credit (LOC).

All your money is parked exactly where it has the greatest return – in the loan itself. And it stayed there until you needed to pay a bill or buy some groceries. Sounds great, but for a lot of people, it just didn't work. It definitely wasn't the maths that caused them to fail. It was the practical implementation.

## Going Backwards

Despite grand plans to make this system work, too many Aussies lacked one vital ingredient.

Discipline.

Using this system required quite a bit of willpower, which many borrowers lacked. The loan itself was almost always a perpetual interest-only account, meaning borrowers could spend every single extra dollar they had paid, bringing the balance right back up to the original limit.

As bad as the old-fashioned 30-year steam train was, at least it was getting paid off slowly. Not the LOC. You could borrow $500,000, but if you spent all the money you put into the loan, then 10 years later the balance would still be $500,000.

All of this contributed to the LOC going the way of the dodo around 2015.

What are your thoughts on this product? It makes sense, right? Put all your income into the loan to reduce your daily balance. Do your shopping and pay your bills from the home loan itself. What's the modern equivalent?

## The Modern All-in-One Loan

If you are reading this book and you are also on TikTok, Facey, or Insta, I can almost guarantee you've seen ads by so-called finfluencers inviting you to a webinar and guaranteeing you'll be debt-free in no time if you register.

The pitch will be some bullshit about the secret the banks don't want you to know and that your current mortgage broker is too lazy to teach you. Getting in on this revolutionary movement will only cost you $3k, which you'll get back in the first couple of months through saved interest.

Let me save you some time and money.

This is what they teach you.

- Use an all-in-one home loan. (They would definitely recommend the old Line of Credit if it was still around).
- Buy an investment property (ideally from the same people running the course).

We will visit the investment property idea later. For now, let's focus on the modern all-in-one loan and what it looks like. An all-in-one loan is not some revolutionary product the banks are hiding from you.

It is just a normal basic home loan that allows you to make unlimited extra repayments and the ability to redraw that money when you need it.

The way it works best is when income is paid directly into it, immediately reducing the balance on which interest is calculated.

Some basic loans allow you to BPAY bills out of the loan itself, but most won't. So, when you have to pay bills or buy groceries, you redraw some of the available funds from the loan to your transaction account and do your spending from there.

How it works:

### Step 1

Get your employer to deposit your income directly into your home loan. This immediately reduces the balance that interest is calculated on.

### Step 2

Keep that money in the home loan for as long as possible. The lower the balance, the less daily interest is charged. The more days the money is in there, the more days you are paying less interest.

### Step 3

Redraw money from the home loan to the transaction account when you need to pay bills and buy groceries. When you take this money out, the home loan balance goes up and therefore daily interest goes up as well. So only redraw what you need.

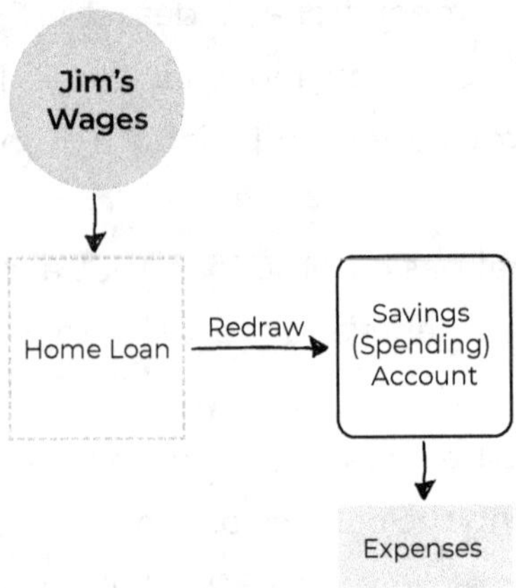


**Pros:**

Income paid directly into the loan reduces the balance that daily interest is calculated from that day onwards.

**Cons:**

You typically can't spend from this loan, so you'll need to keep a transaction account to redraw into and spend from there. Money sitting in this transaction account is not working as hard as money sitting in the loan.

So how do we keep as much money as possible in the home loan for as long as possible, without having to redraw it into a transaction account that doesn't pay us any interest?

Enter the most dangerous hack in this book!

## The 55-Day Interest-Free Credit Card

There were a lot of home loan spruikers in the early 2000s. They were almost boiler-room setups with a team of telemarketers scheduling appointments for the salespeople to go out and convince people like Shaz and Baz that with a few changes to their cash flow and at the super-low cost of $7,500, they could pay their home loan off in seven years.

All they were actually selling was the old Line of Credit or an All-In-One loan, a budgeting spreadsheet, and a revolutionary way of using a credit card (i.e. using it the way it is supposed to be used).

## HACK #5

***Use an interest-free credit card***

How does this process work?

### Step 1

Get your employer to direct all your salary into the home loan.

This immediately reduces the balance that interest is calculated on.

### Step 2

Keep that money there for as long as possible.

### Step 3

Do all your spending on a 55-day interest-free credit card.

Instead of spending your own money, which increases the balance of the home loan, use the bank's money to pay your bills and do your shopping and then pay this back on the last possible day before interest is calculated.

The 55-day interest-free credit card is a gimmick. If you use it properly, the card issuer doesn't make any money out of you.

So, they do everything in their power to ensure you don't use it correctly. As soon as you stuff up, they are beating you over the head with a 21% interest rate.

So don't stuff up.

### Step 4

Pay the credit card back on the last possible day.

The credit card issuer says, "Here is a credit card you can use for all your daily expenditure. If you pay it back within 55 days, we won't charge you a cent of interest."

The best way to do this would be to set up a direct debit to automatically pay the credit card closing balance in full on the due date. Not a day early nor a day late. Not a dollar more nor a dollar less than what is required to avoid having to pay interest on the card.

Some people did make this system work and were able to pay their debts off significantly faster than they otherwise would have. But a lot of people didn't. In fact, some of them went backwards. I am not ashamed to say that I am one of those people.

I know a lot about finance, and I do NOT use a credit card. I don't know what the psychology is behind it, but for some reason, it's easier for me to spend money on a credit card. I'll put things on a credit card that I would never pay cash for. It makes no sense, but I know that I am not alone.

So the safest credit card for me to have is no credit card.

## SUMMARY

Daily interest calculations mean that even minor, short-term balance drops help.

- Parking your income in your home loan saves more interest than a savings account earns, and the ATO can't tax you on it.
- The Line of Credit was an extremely flexible home loan that allowed you to deposit your income directly into the loan and to do your spending from it as well. Unfortunately, they don't really exist anymore.
- The modern alternative is to use a basic loan that allows you to make unlimited extra repayments and also allows you to get that money back out again through redraw when you need to pay bills or do your shopping.
- If you are using this system, you'll need to keep a separate transaction account to pay your bills and do your grocery shopping.
- When you need to spend money, you redraw the available funds in the home loan into the transaction account.
- Using a 55-day interest free credit card allow you to keep your money in the home loan longer, but it comes with its own set of risks.

CHAPTER TEN

# Level Up – Cash Flow For Winners

## A Traditional Cash Flow with Benefits

By now, you know how daily interest is calculated and that saving interest has a far greater return than earning interest. This means you understand that the best place for any savings to be sitting – even just a small amount – is actually in your home loan. The products in the market at the moment that allow us to do that are clunky.

Redraw means that the extra money sitting in the home loan is not readily accessible. You need to leave some cash in your day-to-day transaction account to pay for your living expenses, and unfortunately, that balance is not earning interest nor saving interest. If you do redraw from your home loan, your ever-reliable bank will sometimes charge you for the privilege of accessing your own money.

You now also know how the old-fashioned line of credit works, but also how it is dangerous. A line of credit allows you to have your salary directly deposited into the home loan, and this immediately reduces the balance that daily interest is calculated on. Getting it back out is easy, as this is a home loan that is a transaction account as well.

But this is where the problem lies, and if you aren't a complete tightarse and know where every cent of your money goes, there's a good chance that a line of credit could be as bad for your financial health as a diet of sugary, deep-fried food is for your physical health.

Surely there is a better way?

Worry not, for the debt merchants of Australia have you covered. They have a fantastic product that provides all the benefits of the above loans, but without the dangers and drawbacks.

I know, right?

Why would they give us a product that benefits us and not them and their shareholders?

Well, providing a really useful product and actually educating people on how to set it up and use it properly are two very different things.

## HACK #6

### *Use an Offset Account*

Let's take two steps back and look at a simplified version of the typical cash flow. Income is deposited into a transaction account that pays no interest. From there, bills are paid, cash is withdrawn, and the loan repayment is made. Pretty standard stuff.

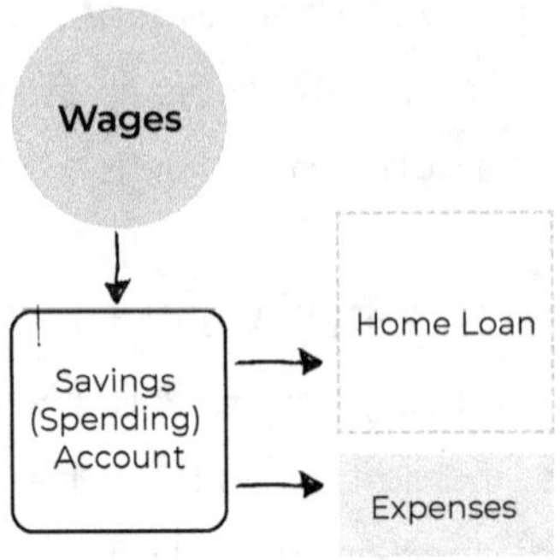


The obvious problem with this cash flow is that you are not earning any interest on the savings, and at the same time, your home loan is at its highest possible balance, meaning daily interest is as high as it can be. Happy bankers.

Wouldn't it be good if you could keep your money in your savings account and also get the interest savings benefits that you would if the money was in the home loan?

Hello, offset account.

An offset account is not a home loan. It is a transaction account that is attached to the home loan. You can have a standard home loan with your repayments set up to come out monthly, fortnightly, or weekly from your savings account.

But this transaction account does not attract any interest on the money sitting in it.

The benefit is that every day when the bank calculates your daily interest amount, they don't calculate it on just the balance of the home loan. Instead, they calculate it on the balance of the home loan **less** the balance of the savings account.

If your home loan balance is $500,000 and you have $5,000 sitting in your offset account, then the bank can only charge you interest on $495,000.

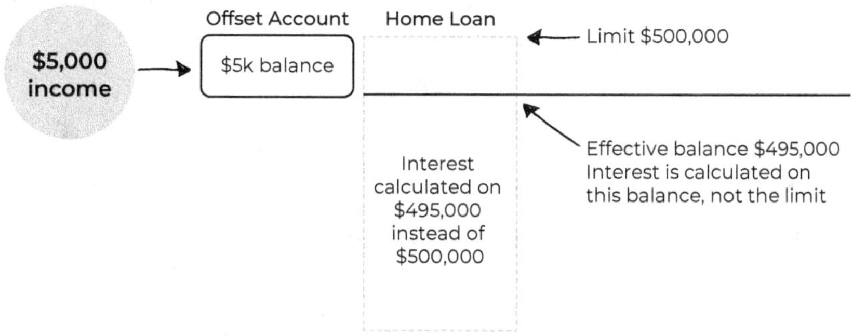


So, money sitting in an offset account is mathematically the same as having money sitting in the home loan. Instead of parking your money in the home loan itself, you are parking it in an account that kind of overlaps the home loan. The outcome is the same, which is reduced interest.

## Offset vs All-in-One

Mathematically, both these loans have the same interest savings benefit. You are using all of your income to reduce the balance that daily interest is calculated on in the home loan. With the all-in-one or line of credit loans, your income is deposited directly into the home loan, immediately reducing the balance that daily interest is calculated on.

With an offset account, your income is deposited into an account that overlaps the home loan. The balance of the offset account is subtracted from the balance of the home loan before interest is calculated.

Both systems focus on the fact that when you have debt, it is better to save interest than earn interest.

The offset account is exactly the same as your day-to-day account. Your income gets paid into it, and you have a debit card attached to it, so you can get cash out of any ATM, tap and go at Coles, and BPAY bills from it.

An all-in-one loan **IS** a loan. An offset account **is not**.

An offset account is simply a normal transaction account that is attached to a home loan, so this gives us two levels of possible hacks. We can hack the home loan, and we can hack the offset account.

The first thing we can do is set the home loan up with those kindergarten debt-reduction tips from the bank.

### Employ Hack #1

You can choose to pay more regularly, and in this case, I'd suggest that the repayments for the loan align with your income. If you get paid weekly, make your loan repayments weekly. Same goes for fortnightly or monthly.

### Employ Hack #2

Pay more than the minimum. Even though the bank will initially set up your loan repayments at the minimum amount, you can easily increase your minimum repayment amount by filling in a direct debit form and nominating your desired repayment amount.

### Employ Hack #6

Meanwhile, whatever money is left sitting in your offset account is being subtracted from the home loan balance that interest is calculated on. The more money in your offset account, the less interest you pay on the home loan, so the idea here is to grow the balance of your offset account as much as possible.

So, what happens when you start crushing it, and you find your offset balance increasing handsomely? You've got $20k sitting in your offset account, which is great, but you're also a bit worried that you have ATM access to that money.

Fear not. You can easily transfer that $20,000 from your offset account to the home loan to keep it a little more out of sight, out of mind.

Mathematically, it doesn't matter where your money sits. Interest is calculated on the balance of the home loan and offset account, so if your money is sitting in the offset or you make extra repayments into the home loan, in terms of how interest is calculated, it makes absolutely no difference.

### Money Sitting in an Offset Account

Loan Balance: $500k

Offset Balance: $20k

Balance that interest is calculated on: $480k

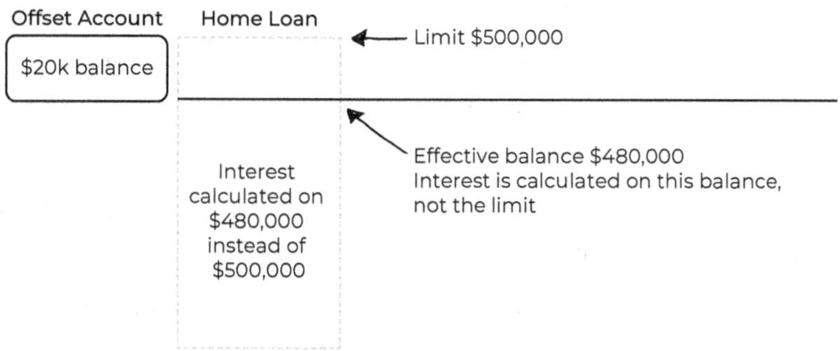

**Money Sitting in the Home Loan Rather Than in the Offset Account**

Loan Balance: $480k

Available Redraw: $20k

Offset Balance: $0

Balance that interest is calculated on: $480k

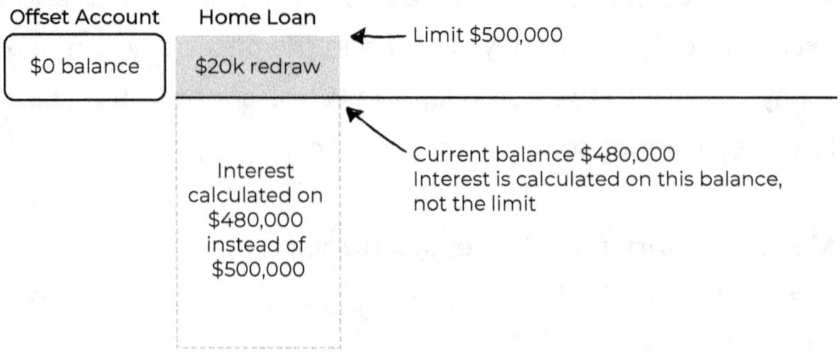


If the car blows up or your favourite child needs some serious orthodontic work to get that million-dollar smile back, then you can redraw the funds from the home loan back into the offset account. In terms of interest calculations, it really doesn't matter.

However, money sitting in a transaction account has a habit of getting spent. For some people, it screams at them, "Get me outta here." For others, it's just following a natural law that available money gets spent.

## Parkinson's Law

Are you most productive when you have a deadline to meet? Do you suffer wild bouts of procrastination when you have plenty of time on your hands? You're not alone.

Cyril Northcote Parkinson feels you. He said, "Work expands so as to fill the time available for its completion."* This concept is known as Parkinson's Law.

Shit gets done when you're busy, right? This is why if you want something done, you should ask a busy person to do it.

A job that would take you ten minutes to do when you're pumped up will often take you an hour to do if you have that hour free.

This law is absolutely true for the vast majority of humans. It's also an excellent argument for the four-day work week.

And, yep, we can apply Parkinson's Law to money. People tend to spend ALL the money that is available to them. If they get a pay rise, instead of saving that extra money, they spend it.

Their lifestyle adapts to the extra income, and they eat out more, go on bigger and better holidays, and buy fancy boutique beers that come in a four-pack instead of XXXX Gold.

And the opposite is true. If income decreases, sacrifices are made and discretionary spending is cut. Fewer dinners out, more bangers and mash, cask wine.

Let's look at a hack that utilises Parkinson's Law.

## Hybrid Offset and Redraw

No, I'm not talking about cars.

Over the years and the thousands of times I've presented these diagrams to my clients, there have been countless examples of borrowers understanding the differences and being attracted to both hacks – park your money in the home loan, and park your money in the offset account. Their thinking usually goes along the following lines:

* www.economist.com/news/1955/11/19/parkinsons-law

- The offset account is convenient. It gives me easy access to my cash, as it operates like any standard transaction account.
- But money in my day-to-day account has a tendency to get spent.
- If I'm not consistently increasing my offset balance, then I'm not really decreasing my home loan.
- Maybe parking the money in the home loan is better, but then it's a hassle to access the money, and I may be charged fees to do so.
- If only there was a way I could combine the benefits of both.

I have you covered.

## HACK #7

### *Hybrid Offset and Redraw (Parkinson's Law)*

This is almost like a forced savings to ensure that even if you spend all your offset balance during a standard pay cycle, some of your income is going directly onto the loan itself to help reduce debt.

As explained above, whether money is sitting in the offset account or in redraw, the outcome is exactly the same in terms of interest saved.

Here's our standard offset cash flow:

- All income goes into the offset account.

- The minute your income hits the offset account, the balance that interest is calculated on in the home loan reduces by the exact same amount.
- Over the next month, the offset balance gets spent on your household expenses, so the balance that interest is calculated on in the home gradually increases.

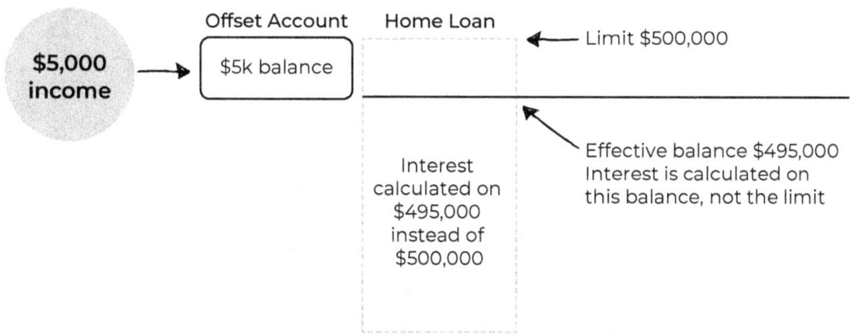


And here's how we can tweak that a little. Instead of putting all your income into the offset account, work out how much you should be able to save each month if you reined in some of those costly habits and got your payroll officer to split your payslip and deposit a certain amount each pay cycle directly into the home loan and the rest into the offset account.

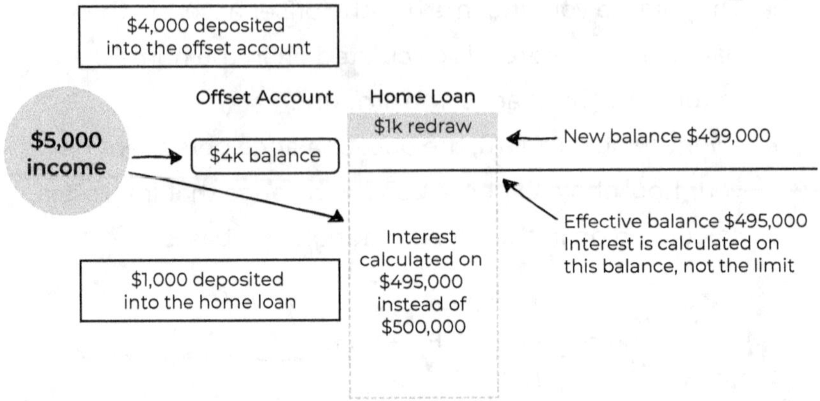


Ideally, every pay cycle, a certain amount of money is paid directly into the home loan, where it is a little more out of sight, out of mind. The rest of the money goes into the offset account and hopefully is enough to get you through until the next payday.

Remember the calculations we did earlier on looking at how quickly a debt could be repaid if you made an extra $1,000 payment per month? The $500k debt at 6% interest would be gone after 16 years, a little over half of the original term. It would also save you over $290,000 in interest over that time.

Extreme example, I know, but this is what the above cash flow could achieve.

For couples, you could put this on steroids.

## HACK #8

### *Parkinson's Law for Couples*

This hack is fairly simple, and obviously, it is not going to be for everyone.

If you have two incomes, like Bazza and Shazza, and you can live off one of the wages alone, put 100% of the other one into the home loan.

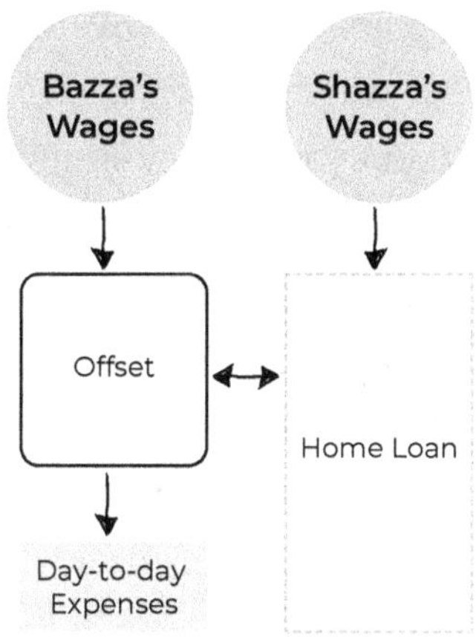


All of Shazza's wages are going into the home loan, while Bazza's goes into the offset. Hopefully, they can live on Bazza's income alone and not need to redraw any of the extra funds sitting in the loan. But that option is always there if needed.

This is going to be impossible for most people if they are on a single wage or their living expenses cannot be covered by one wage alone.

### *Savings vs Available Balance*

Imagine the difference in spending habits if the banks just changed some of the terminology that they use. When you get cash out of an ATM, the receipt shows an "Available Balance", which is a thinly veiled way of saying, "Spend me." What do we think when something is available?

A hotel will promote the fact that parking is available. Mechanics will assure you that a courtesy car is available while your car is being serviced. Gift wrapping is available at many shopping centres before Christmas. These are conveniences. They suggest we think about taking advantage of this positive, beneficial service.

What does it say about your money sitting in a bank account? You get $50 out of the ATM, and it tells you that you still have $2,342 available. Available to spend. "So, spend me. What could you buy with that money? Don't you need a ...?"

Imagine if the banks implemented a very simple change to this wording. Imagine if instead of being told what your available balance is whenever you look at your savings account, it just said "Savings".

Your ATM receipt would look like this:

Withdrawal: $50

Savings: $2,342

I'm no psychologist, but I reckon this would have a significant impact on many people. Chances of this becoming a reality? Somewhere between Buckley's and none.

## CHAPTER ELEVEN

# Are You a Future Landlord?

### This Part Is a Must-Read

By now you should be attracted to one of the above options. Whether it is redraw, an offset account, or a combination of a couple of them, they all provide a superior cash flow compared to the old-fashioned standard loan and, used correctly, will help you pay off your loan faster by paying less interest.

A correctly used all-in-one loan by a disciplined borrower is just as good as an offset account. For some people, the psychological and emotional benefit of seeing their debt reduce is a greater motivator than seeing their savings increase in an offset account. However, if there is even a slight chance that your property could become an investment property in the future, then, put simply – an offset account is a no-brainer. Unless you want to run the risk of the ATO going through your dirty laundry, that is.

While you are living in your home, there is no taxation benefit from the loan. You usually can't claim any of the interest as a tax deduction, just as you can't claim the rates, insurances, and upkeep as a tax deduction. However, if the property was a rental that you were earning an income from, then there would be quite a few tax deductions that you could and should claim.

But while you are living in the property, then as a rule, any associated costs of the property cannot be claimed as a tax deduction. So, it makes sense that while it is your principal place of residence, you try to smash the debt as quickly as possible. The quicker you pay off the debt, the less interest you will pay and the sooner you will be debt-free. Great, right?

Now I am going to explain the ins and outs of investment properties and negative gearing, and how some people utilise these in a way that allows them to reduce their debt faster, but not until Chapter Fourteen. It might pay to come back and read this section again after you have a thorough understanding of negative gearing.

But for now, the important thing to know is that if you do have an investment property, the interest you pay on the investment loan is tax-deductible.

And the interest you pay on your home loan for the house you are living in is NOT tax-deductible.

If you have both these kinds of debts, you logically want to smash the one that doesn't give you a tax benefit. Simple.

If you don't own an investment property, you are probably thinking that this has nothing to do with you and that you should just be smashing your debt as quickly as possible. And I'd agree with you. But is it possible that the property you are now living in could become an investment at some point in the future?

Is there even a slight chance that you may want to upgrade in the future or buy in another region if work takes you there? Would you want to hold onto your current property and rent it out?

Smashing your debt now will mean that you have less tax deductibility when you rent it out in the future. This invariably means you will pay more tax than if the loan was fully drawn. So, what do you do? Deliberately not reduce your debt now and pay more interest while it is a bad debt in the hope that you will save some tax when it does become an investment? That's not such a great idea.

Well, how about just pulling the extra funds you've got sitting in redraw when it becomes an investment? That way, you have kept the loan balance as low as possible while you're living in the home, and have increased it when it is tax-deductible.

Good in theory, but just wait until the tax man sees what you've done.

Extra money you have paid off the home loan is considered to be a permanent reduction of the principal. Deliberately increasing this and claiming the increase as a tax deduction is okay – provided you used the redrawn funds for the purpose of the investment property. If you just take the money out so you can claim the highest amount of interest on the loan and deposit it in a savings account – then unfortunately, you are not following the school rules. The ATO looks very poorly on this practice. In fact, they call it tax avoidance. You don't want to do that.

***Conundrum:*** how do you reduce the interest you pay while it is a bad debt, and then legally maximise the interest when it becomes a good debt? Answer: offset account.

Money sitting in an offset account reduces the balance that interest is calculated on in the home loan, but it doesn't actually reduce the home loan balance itself. At all times, there are really three balances. The home loan balance, the offset balance, and the effective balance; which equals the home loan balance minus the offset balance.

Building up your savings in the offset account has the same effect as having that same amount sitting in the home loan as redraw. The benefit is that if you take your money out of the offset account, it has no effect on the balance of the home loan. What it does have an effect on is the balance that interest is calculated on, but right now, that is not something that the ATO is concerned about.

Long story short:

- Your home loan for the property you live in is bad debt. You cannot claim the interest as a tax deduction.
- Interest on your investment loan is tax-deductible, so it makes sense to maximise this amount to get the greatest taxation benefit.
- If you make extra payments off the loan while you live there, you can't just redraw those funds and increase the loan balance and claim all the interest as a tax deduction when the property becomes an investment.
- An offset account allows you to reduce the effective balance of the home loan while you are living there, then maximise the interest when it becomes an investment property.

CHAPTER TWELVE

# The Multiple Offset Movement

## If One Glass of Red Wine a Day Is Good for You, Then Surely Two Is Even Better

The only thing better than an offset account is several offset accounts.

**HACK #9**

*Use multiple offset accounts.*

We often see the cash flow where a client has multiple savings accounts – all for different purposes. There's the main account that their income is paid into and that they use as their day-to-day account. Then they have another account that they transfer money into to pay their bills. This is smart. Instead of hoping they have enough money to pay the rates and insurances when they come up, these clients squirrel enough money away each pay cycle to cover all their bills for the year.

Some also have a Christmas account, a holiday account, an account for the rich uncle to deposit his generous birthday gifts into for the kids. It's common for people to have multiple savings accounts, and it works, as it allows them to put money aside for different purposes and to easily track it.

The problem, though, is that in most cases you get paid absolutely no interest on these balances, and if you do, it's pretty minuscule. Then you have to pay tax on it. Ideally, those funds would be better off sitting in the offset account, as it would be reducing the balance that interest is calculated on in the home loan. But that sucks, because if all the money is in one account, you can't track how much you have available for the different categories that you used to have clearly delineated.

Here's a revolutionary idea. Why not just have multiple offset accounts? That way, you can separate your savings into your various categories that make sense to you. The balance of all the accounts put together comes off your home loan, and interest is calculated on the rest. I know what you're thinking. That's not really such an earth-shattering, revolutionary idea. And I agree. But try to convince a bank of that.

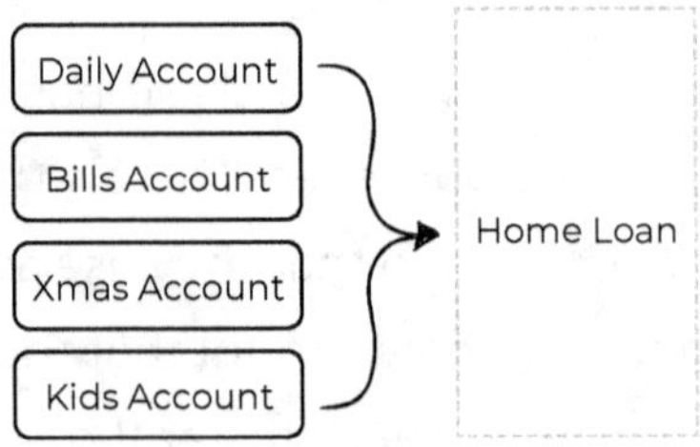

The total balance of all offset accounts is coming off the home loan balance.

Unfortunately, not all banks offer offset accounts, let alone multiple offset accounts. More and more banks are introducing the idea, but they are still in the minority.

## Comparing Apples With Oranges

### Basic Loans vs Fancy Loans

By now, I'm probably sounding as if I'm the guy who invented offset accounts. Yep, I sing their praises. In my opinion, there is no more powerful way of reducing the interest you pay on the loan, while enjoying so many positive features and benefits, than using an offset account. If there is even a slight chance the property might become an investment in the future, a basic loan with redraw has nothing on a good loan with an offset account.

Except for the cost.

Very often, the only way you can get an offset account is if you take out the bank's "professional package". The banks don't just want your home loan. They want your home loan, your transaction accounts, your credit card, your insurances, and any other banking product they can sell you, so they offer you the whole suite of banking products for one annual fee that is often between $150 and $400. The fewer accounts you have with other banks, the less chance the bank has of losing you, and so they offer you a package that covers all your banking needs. This is like building a fence around their customers.

In most cases, this pro-pack will also come with a generous interest rate discount, especially if you borrow heaps of money. The more you borrow, the lower your rate becomes. However, it might not be the lowest-rate home loan they offer. In some cases, their basic loan with no fees has a lower interest rate, but unfortunately, you don't get the offset account. In these cases, the basic loan looks far more attractive, and very often clients will save more money than if they had an offset account. But not always.

Let's look at a simple example. Shaz and Baz are sick of their bank and are looking to refinance their $500,000 home loan. They are tossing up between the basic loan at 5.8% and no ongoing fees, or the pro-pack at 6% with a $375 annual fee. Based on the assumption that they make no extra repayments on the basic loan and have no savings in the offset account, the basic loan will save them $1,000 in interest over the year. When you factor in the annual fee, this makes the pro-pack with offset account $1,375 more expensive per year than the basic loan, all things being equal.

But all things are not equal.

Baz and Shaz will always have some sort of balance in their offset account if they go with the pro-pack, but how much would they need to save at least $1,375 per year so that the offset is a stronger choice than the basic loan?

$22,916?

If they had $22,916 in an offset account, then they would be saving 6% of that amount on their home loan every year, which is $1,375.

This is the question that they need to ask themselves: "Do I expect to keep an average balance of around $22,916 in my offset account at all times?"

If so, then the pro-pack at the slightly higher cost could be the way to go. If not, then maybe they should just stick with the basic loan.

## Should I Fix?

This is one of the banks' go-to plays that makes them some serious dough. Before we dive into whether fixing is a good idea or not, let's first look at what it actually is.

We have two types of interest rates in Australia – fixed and variable. Most people are on variable rate loans, which can fluctuate, especially when the Reserve Bank of Australia (RBA) changes the cash rate.

A fixed rate eliminates your exposure to these fluctuations by locking in a rate that is guaranteed not to change for anywhere between one and five years.

If your rate stays the same, then so does your monthly repayment. Sounds good, right?

Why would you fix? There are two reasons why people choose to fix their interest rate.

The right reason. And the wrong reason.

### The Wrong Reason

This reasoning is akin to gambling. I don't know about you, but I work way too hard for my money to gamble it away. When the fixed rates appear very low, and you can't imagine them getting any lower, you'd be mad not to fix, right?

If the only way is up, then I'll lock in a crazy low fixed rate now and laugh at all the plebs who stayed variable when the inevitable increases hit.

This is crystal ball thinking, and the opposite could well be true. Look at how low rates got during the pandemic. Imagine if you fixed your rate in February 2020 and locked in what seemed like a fairly attractive 3.99% rate for five years, and within a few months, the same bank was offering 1.99% fixed rates.

We do not know what the future holds, so betting on the direction of interest rates is like putting your money on red at the roulette table. The bank is the casino, and the casino always wins. They are simply never going to offer us a product that they are not going to make money on.

## The Right Reason

A great reason to lock in a fixed rate is stability. If you worry about how you will afford your loan repayments if the rate goes up a couple of times, then fixing is a sensible option to consider. With a fixed rate loan, your repayments will not change during that fixed rate period, regardless of what happens to the cash rate and the economy. If this helps you budget your income and sleep well at night, then that is a great reason to fix.

Property investors may also be attracted to fixed rate loans as they allow them to accurately calculate their yields in preparation for the end of the taxation year.

But all that glitters is not gold. Fixing your interest rate should not be a spur-of-the-moment decision. If you have a fixed rate loan, paying out the loan early by refinancing or selling the home before the end of the fixed rate period can incur significant penalties.

In most cases, how much extra you can pay off the fixed rate loan per year is restricted, which pretty much means that not only is your interest rate fixed, but so is your loan balance. You can't usually have an offset account attached to a fixed rate loan either, so while the interest rate might be attractive, the bells and whistles are often lacking.

## SUMMARY

- Multiple offsets are great for people who love to squirrel their money into different accounts like bills. Holidays and Christmas
- Basic loans with no offset accounts are usually cheaper than professional packages that have them
- Fixed rate loans typically do not allow offset accounts to be attached to them, so factor this in before you fix

## CHAPTER THIRTEEN

# Fees

## Because Banks Don't Make Enough Money from Interest

There is always that one child at a kid's birthday party, the one who hangs on to the parcel the longest, hoping the music will stop before they pass it. The parents among us will know who this child is. The one right there when the presents are being opened, and though seemingly impossible, they manage to squeeze themselves between your kid and their present to be the first to see what it is unwrapped.

Of course, they are the first to play with the presents. They complain when the cordial comes out, looking at the kid next to them and wailing that "she got more than me". The party pies don't even have time to hit the table before they've got one in each hand, storing the second in their mouth just in case they are the last pies on the face of the earth. After inhaling their slice of cake and the leftovers of a few others, cleaning out the lolly bowl, and finding the box of party favours and helping themselves to two bags, they still come up to you and plead, "Johnny's Mum, I'm hungry."

This kid's middle name is "Greed" and is precisely the reason you sit your little cherub down after the party and declare that hell will freeze over before you ever host another birthday party.

Now, picture the CEO of your bank sitting with his board of directors and lamenting their lot in life.

> *"Gentlemen, we don't seem to be making enough money. Yeah, we calculate interest daily, and most people will pay us double their loan amount over the life of the loan, but it just doesn't seem enough. If only we could gouge a little more out of them."*

How can they get a pie in each hand and one in the mouth before the plate even hits the table?

Fees. And lots of them.

### Application Fee

Many banks will charge an application fee, which can be anywhere from $150 to over $1,000, depending on the bank and the loan.

### Monthly Fee

Then there are the monthly fees.

> *"Yes, we charge you over $800 in interest every month, but we'd also like to charge you an extra $10 every month for having an account with us."*

In this day and age of automated technology, exactly what does an account-keeping fee pay for?

### Annual Fee

This is like a monthly fee but charged annually, so you don't notice it as often.

### Package Fee

The banks don't just want your home loan. They want your transaction accounts, your credit card, and your insurances as well, so they offer you a package that includes all these products in exchange for one single annual fee. If you pay this fee, then there should be no other fees on your banking products – no account-keeping fees and no credit card annual fee.

Very often, paying the package fee is the only way that you can get the all-important offset account. It also used to give you the lowest interest rates as the banks would give the greatest discounts off the standard variable rate on this product.

### Redraw Fee

> *"Oh, you've paid extra off your home loan and want to get some of it out to pay for an unexpected expense? No worries – we have a fee for that."*

This fee is probably the one that gets my back up the most. The bank will actually charge you a fee to get your own money out.

Moral of the story? Beware of fees.

A quick way to check if a loan has lots of fees is to look at the comparison rate. There's a lot I don't like about comparison rates, but they are very useful in showing if a loan has high fees or not.

## Why Comparison Rates Are Shit

You know as well as I do that what is advertised and what you actually get can be two very different things. Think hamburgers. The picture looks amazing – fluffy bun, juicy meat patty, perfect leaf of crispy lettuce, slices of tomato and melted cheese sneaking out from under the bun in complete symmetry. A piece of art.

And then you unwrap your lunch, only to find what appears to be a squashed, hairless mammal that is yet to be scientifically classified. Of course, it tastes way better than it looks.

But we expect this, right? We know it is going to look like it did an eight-hour shift in your back pocket before unwrapping, so it's not a rude shock. The same can't be said of other products and services. If, for example, you want to buy an airline ticket, you'd assume the advertised price would buy you... an airline ticket. And you'd be wrong.

My wife recently went through the ordeal of trying to book something as simple as a flight from Brisbane to Sydney. An online site was advertising the early flight for $69, which seemed like a bargain, so she naturally clicked on the book button before the airline could realise this was a steal.

Ready to enter the card details, the auto booking system then asked her if she would like to bring any luggage, because ...

"That's another $20. So just tick this box, and we'll add it to your bill ...

We only accept credit card payment, so will that be credit card or credit card today? Oh, you're paying by credit card? We have a credit card fee of 2.5%. Just tick the box, please ...

Almost there. Now you have your flight ticket, would you also like a seat? No, you can't stand in the aisle, so you'll have to make a choice from the following ...

Platinum gets you the bulkhead. Gold gets you a window. Silver for the aisle, and Bronze for a middle seat. Bronze? That's $15. Please tick the box and hit next."

You get the picture – $69 is a steal, and that is definitely not the price you are going to pay at the end of the process.

I know this will come as a shock, but banks were once guilty of this kind of misleading advertising. They would offer crazy low interest rates, and in fine print, they would disclose the exorbitant fees they charge.

Or they would proudly proclaim: "NO MONTHLY FEES! $3,500 annual fee.

And for this reason, the government got a little annoyed and decided to make the banks display a comparison rate in their advertising.

Ideally, this rate would reflect the true cost of the loan by factoring in the range of fees you'd be likely to pay over the life of the loan, as well as the ongoing interest, and then translate this into a percentage figure. That's why you'll often see what seems like a crazy low interest rate advertised, followed by a comparison rate that is markedly different.

When we look at an advertised rate and a comparison rate side by side, if there is a large difference between them, then that usually means the specific loan product being advertised has a shitload of fees. If they are really similar, it means the product doesn't have many fees at all. Simple.

Not really. Unfortunately, the comparison rates that you see in advertising can be extremely misleading.

First of all, the comparison rates that you see advertised are based on a loan amount of $150,000 to be paid off over 25 years. So, if your loan is a touch higher than this amount (I'm looking at you, Sydneysiders), then how accurate is this comparison rate going to be?

The comparison rate does not include any redraw fees and also does not factor in the benefits of an offset account or funds sitting in redraw. If your credit card annual fee is waived because it is part of your home loan package, this saving is also not considered.

## A True Loan Comparison

A much better way of comparing loans is to look at the total cost over the life of the loan and factor in the fees that you are most likely to pay and leave out the ones you won't. Let's compare what that looks like using the following loans as examples.

| Loan Type | Amount | Interest Rate | Application Fee | Monthly Fee | Annual Fee |
|---|---|---|---|---|---|
| Basic | $500,000 | 6.0% | $1,000 | $0 | $0 |
| Standard Variable | $500,000 | 6.2% | $0 | $10 | $0 |
| Professional Package (Offset) | $500,000 | 6.1% | $0 | $0 | $395 |

If you make the minimum repayment over the life of the loan for these accounts, this is what you'd end up paying. For the basic loan, not only would you pay the $500k that you owe, but during those 30 years, you'd also pay $579,191 worth of interest and $1,000 in fees. Your $500k home loan will actually cost you $1,080,191.

| Product Name | Basic | Offset Package | Standard Variable |
|---|---|---|---|
| Loan Amount | $500,000 | $500,000 | $500,000 |
| Interest Rate(s) | 6.00%<br>30 yrs (var) | 6.10%<br>30 yrs (var) | 6.20%<br>30 yrs (var) |
| Repayments | $2,998/month<br>30 yrs | $3,030/month<br>30 yrs | $3,062/month<br>30 yrs |
| App Fee | $1,000 | | |
| Monthly Fee | | | $10 |
| Annual Fee | | $395 | |
| Total Interest | $579,191 | $590,791 | $602,444 |
| Total Monthly Fees | | | $3,600 |
| Total of Annual Fees | | $11,850 | |
| Total Setup Costs | $1,000 | | |
| Loan Term | 30 yrs | 30 yrs | 30 yrs |
| Total Loan Cost | $580,191 | $602,641 | $606,044 |
| Difference | | $3,404 | $25,853 |

Because the offset package has a slightly higher interest rate and an annual fee of $395, which repeats 30 times during the loan (adding up to a whopping $11,850), the actual cost of this loan is $3,404 more than the basic loan over the 30 years.

And the standard loan at the higher interest rate with the $10 per month fee works out to be $25,853 more expensive over 30 years than the basic loan.

Change any of these variables, and the total loan cost calculation will change. This is a far more accurate way of comparing loans than relying on a haphazard comparison rate.

Why? Because it is an actual comparison.

## SUMMARY

- Home loan fees can add up to a lot of money over the life of a loan
- Comparison rates were designed to make it easier to see if a bank had outrageous fees. They are helpful, but flawed.
- Do a real comparison when tossing up between two lenders by calculating the entire interest and all fees over the loan term.

# PART 4

# INVESTING IN DEBT REDUCTION

**IN THIS SECTION, YOU'LL LEARN:**

The difference between good debt and bad debt.

How tax is calculated.

How investors try to reduce the tax they pay.

The cash flow reality of being a landlord.

## BEFORE WE GET OURSELVES AUDITED

As this book was heading off to print, the Australian Government announced proposed changes to negative gearing and Capital Gains Tax (CGT) rules for investment properties.

At the time of writing, these changes have been announced but not yet passed into legislation. That said, it appears highly likely the government will have the numbers to get the changes through Parliament.

If legislated, the proposed rules are expected to apply to existing residential properties purchased after Tuesday 12 May 2026.

So here's the important bit:

**The strategies and explanations in this section remain accurate for:**

- **investment properties purchased before 12 May 2026, and**
- **newly built properties purchased after this date.**

**However, some of the tax outcomes discussed may no longer apply to existing residential properties purchased after 12 May 2026 if the legislation passes in its current form.**

Now before you throw the book into the nearest body of water, understand this:

The core concepts in these chapters are still incredibly important.

Cashflow matters.
Loan structure matters.
Offset accounts matter.
Tax deductibility still matters.
Debt recycling still matters.

Governments can change tax rules. They cannot change maths.

The purpose of these chapters is to help you understand how lending, tax deductibility, and cashflow actually work so you can make smarter decisions regardless of what political circus is happening in Canberra this week.

Also, tax law changes more often than a toddler changes favourite foods, so please make sure you get up-to-date advice before making investment decisions.

For the latest updates and resources, head to:
**perch.finance**

CHAPTER FOURTEEN

# Investment Properties

**HACK #10**

*Buy an investment property.*

So, here's a novel idea. Go into more debt as a way of reducing debt. Makes total sense, right?

Seems counterintuitive, but the reality is that this is precisely what many people do. If their calculations pan out, property investors usually intend to buy property and borrow as much as they legally can to do so, and as a result, speed up their debt-reduction goals.

And it works. Provided the calculations pan out ...

And they get good tenants who pay the rent on time ...

And they buy the right property in the right area ...

And the economy chugs along as they had planned ...

And their managing agent actually does their job ...

And their insurer pays out on claims when disaster strikes ...

And their accountant makes sure they aren't claiming anything they're not supposed to ...

And ... you get the idea.

Buying an investment property or a share portfolio *can* help you reduce your debt faster. Key word here is "can". It's possible. You *can* also lose a lot of money.

But if the planets align, investing can help you become debt-free sooner.

Whether you buy property or shares, the calculations and overall strategies are much the same. And as most people are more familiar with property than shares, I'm going to choose the path of least resistance and explain how investing in property works and how it can help some people speed up their debt reduction.

I'll then touch on how the same principles can apply when it comes to shares and a couple of specific hacks relating to them.

## Disclaimer

This is really simplistic, and I'm not going to apologise for that. I'm not going to write *War and Peace* because I know you wouldn't read it if I did.

There are heaps of great books out there that explain investing in property and shares way better than I have in the following pages. So, if this is something you are interested in, get down to the library and learn as much as you can. The following chapter is finger-painting in comparison.

Let me get this very clear from the start. I'll never actively spruik investment properties to my clients, regaling them with stories of how the right investment now could see them sipping margaritas on exotic beaches within a few short years. I will, however, most definitely help educate anyone interested in investing.

## Aussies Love Property (Too Much)

My opinion is that property should be for shelter, which is a basic human right. I'm all for keeping property affordable so that as many individuals and families as possible can secure a house that they can turn into a home. I worry that property is getting less and less affordable for young families.

Take a look at the following graph. It shows wage and property growth between 2000 and 2025. Wages have grown slowly but steadily, but look at how much property has gone up.

Wages and property used to be closely aligned, but now there is virtually no correlation between them. It's my own humble opinion that this divergence is due to the growth in popularity of property investing.

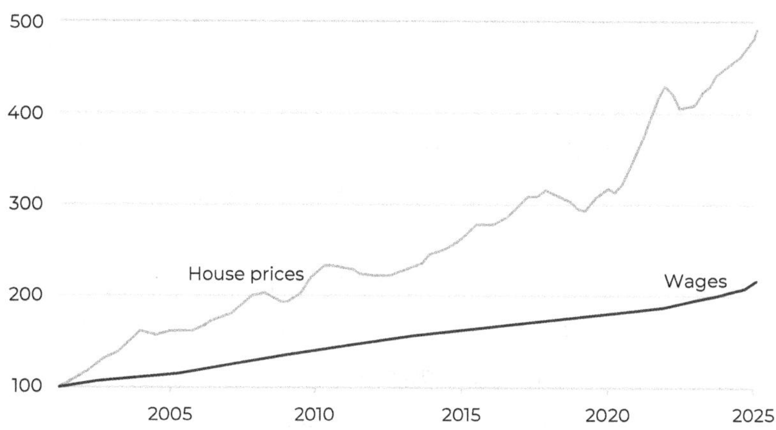


*Values indexed to a common starting point in 2001 for comparison.*
*Source: https://www.abc.net.au/news/2025-11-02/house-prices-climbing-for-generation/105954416*

What has caused property investment to become such an attractive strategy for the average Aussie? A lot of tax benefits is the short answer.

The largest expense when you own an investment property is usually the interest on the loan, which can be claimed as a tax deduction along with the management fees, council rates, and insurances. And then when the property is sold for a profit, the investor only pays tax on 50% of the amount the property has increased in value by.

Unless these rules are changed by future governments, property will likely continue to get even more expensive and out of reach of anyone but the wealthy.

Okay, that's my rant over. I think you get the picture.

The reality is that not everyone can buy a house, and there will always be a market for property owners to rent their properties to tenants. Being a landlord could even be described as noble. As a landlord, you are providing a home at a fair price to a family that may not otherwise be able to afford one, and in return, you are allowed to take advantage of some very attractive tax benefits.

While the rules are there that allow you to reduce your tax, why not use them? Kerry Packer summed it up nicely when questioned about his tax payments during the 1991 Senate Fairfax Inquiry:

> *"Of course, I am minimising my tax. And if anybody in this country doesn't minimise their tax, they want their heads read, because as a government, I can tell you you're not spending it that well that we should be donating extra!"*

I'm not sure about you, but I don't get a lot of enjoyment from paying tax. Don't get me wrong – it's vitally important for our country that everyone who earns a certain level of income pays their fair share of tax so we can continue to have schools, hospitals, and helicopter rides for politicians. However, if there is a way that you can legally reduce the tax that you pay, then you'd be a mug if you didn't use the tax laws to your benefit.

Okay, let's take a step back and start from the beginning.

There are three main ways that buying an investment property can help someone reduce their debt faster.

1. Capital growth.
2. Tax deductions.
3. Cash flow.

## Capital Growth

### Buy Low, Sell High

Buy an asset → Hold onto it while it increases in value → Sell it and use the proceeds to pay off your debt.

Capital growth is simply the gradual, but sometimes rapid, increase in the value of something.

Between having to listen to Len and Stan sharing their hip replacement and coronary bypass war stories at the bowlsy, you've probably also heard how they bought their first home for 3 quid and a tuppence (I have no idea what that means). When they sold it in 1972 for $30,000, they completely paid off the remaining 1 quid and 6 shillings home loan, leaving them with quite the windfall left over.

In today's parlance, Bob's home is worth $500,000, and he owes $400,000.

He buys another $500,000 investment property and borrows $450,000.

Total debt is $850,000 secured by property worth $1,000,000.

Over the next ten years, both properties increase in value by about 7% per year.

Let's just look at the investment property.

| Starting Value | $500,000 |
|---|---:|
| After 1 year | $535,000 |
| After 2 years | $572,450 |
| After 3 years | $612,522 |
| After 4 years | $655,399 |
| After 5 years | $701,277 |

Total capital growth over five years is $201,277.

| After 6 years | $750,366 |
|---|---:|
| After 7 years | $802,892 |
| After 8 years | $859,094 |
| After 9 years | $919,231 |
| After 10 years | $983,577 |

After ten years, the investment property alone is worth nearly $1 million.

And during that time, what has happened to the loans? Unlike the value of the properties, the loans should have decreased, especially if Bob is using the home loan hacks.

Assuming a constant interest rate of 6%, here's how the loans look even if Bob was making the minimum monthly repayment and not using an offset account or any of the other home loan hacks.

| | |
|---|---:|
| Starting Balance | $850,000 |
| After 1 year | $839,562 |
| After 2 years | $828,480 |
| After 3 years | $816,785 |
| After 4 years | $804,224 |
| After 5 years | $776,883 |
| After 6 years | $761,935 |
| After 7 years | $746,065 |
| After 8 years | $729,716 |
| After 9 years | $711,329 |
| After 10 years | $692,338 |

If property increases in value by a steady 7% per year and the home loan interest rate does not fluctuate and stays at exactly 6% (about as likely as me starting an OnlyFans page), Bob could have sold his investment property after seven years and paid off all his debt, including the loan on his home.

It's that simple.

Buy an asset → Hold onto it while it increases in value → Sell it and use the proceeds to pay off your debt.

Sounds too good to be true? Yep. Wait until the tax office gets wind of this.

### Capital Gains Tax

When you make money on an investment, the government will want its cut too. And why shouldn't they? They are responsible for the economic environment that has allowed that capital growth to take place.

When this happens to you, I'm sure you will use a very good

accountant to give you the exact cost. But the equation is fairly basic on the surface.

The difference between what you bought the property for and what you sold it for is the capital gain (or capital loss); 50% of this amount is added to your taxable income in that financial year.

If Bob sells his investment property for $800,000 seven years after buying it for $500,000, he will have achieved a capital gain of $300,000; 50% of that is added to his taxable income that year.

If Bob was earning $80,000 per year before selling the property, he would have been paying about $17,500 per year in tax.

When he sells the investment property and nets a cool $300k, 50% of that – $150k – is added to his taxable income that year. Bob now has to pay tax on $230,000 instead of $80,000.

Tax on $230,000 is $74,167. This is a whopping $56,667 more tax than Bob is used to.

Bob now realises that selling his property after seven years is not going to clear his debt. He may have made $300,000 in capital growth, but after capital gains tax, he gets about $243,333.

And let's not forget that he probably engaged a real estate agent to sell the property and parted with up to $20,000 in commission. His profit is now down to $223,333.

So, after seven years, Bob sells the property for $800,000, which is whittled down to $723,333 after capital gains tax and commission. At the same time, his debt is $746,065. If he uses the whole proceeds from the sale to reduce his debt, he is still left with just under $23,000 of debt.

Based on these projections, maybe Bob should have held on to the property a bit longer, though this would have also resulted in higher capital gains tax and agent commissions, assuming the value of the property increased in that time.

## Ramping It Up – Becoming a Property Mogul

If one investment property can allow Bob to smash out his debt in such a short amount of time, imagine what a few could do?

If you let a salesperson convince you to buy one investment property, you can be damn sure they are already preparing the script to sell you a second and third.

I've attended a fair few investment property presentations, and the magic number for many of them is four. Buy your own home first, then buy another three properties to rent out. When you retire, sell one of them and pay off the debt on the remaining three. Live in one of them, and as there is no debt to continue paying, use the rental income from the other two to fund your retirement, along with your superannuation.

Some people make it work. Some people don't. This strategy is getting very hard to achieve now with banks making it more and more difficult to borrow money when you already have several properties along with a sizeable level of debt.

Like anything, having a strategy attached to capital growth has its pros and cons.

## Capital Growth Pros

**Property *usually* goes up in value.**

This increase is passive in that you don't have to go out and work for it. Think about a standard job like a police officer. The cop has to go to work and complete her shift before she gets paid. She is basically exchanging her time and labour for money. The less time she spends at work, the less she is paid. The more she works, the more she earns. This is active.

Capital growth is passive. Most properties increase in value over time, whether you work 12 hours a day or sit at home and engage in a bong-a-thon. When you sell the property, you get to keep most of the difference between what you bought it for and what you sold it for, with very little labour expended.

### Property loans usually decrease.

While the value of the property is going up, the mortgage is coming down. This increases the equity in the property, so you walk away with more when you sell it.

## Capital Growth Cons

### Boom and bust.

Property simply does not increase in value by 7% per year, every year without fail. Sometimes it increases by double that amount in one year. Sometimes it falls in value and takes years to get back to where it was. Assuming your investment will be worth a specific amount in X years is simply wishful thinking.

The same goes for interest rates. There's no way that they will stay at the same rate for several years with no change. Therefore, it's important to remember that projections are just that, and to also complete projections that assume lower growth and higher interest rates.

CHAPTER FIFTEEN

# Investments and Tax

## Tax Deductions

The second way investing in property can help you reduce debt is by reducing your tax.

We all love a tax refund, right? It's nice to get a lump sum in the second half of the year. For most people, it's not a massive amount – a few hundred dollars because they claimed some laundry expenses.

Imagine you usually get $200 a year tax refund, and then one year you get $5,000. I'm hoping you will do the right thing with that money and park it in your offset account because if you do this, you will be debt-free sooner than if you spend it.

This is what buying an investment property can do.

While you sit back and wait for your investment property value to grow, there are a few things you and your accountant can do to make sure you aren't paying more tax than you need to. Ideally, paying less tax means you may be able to make additional repayments on your loans – leading to faster debt reduction.

When people talk about investment property, it's almost inevitable that the term "negative gearing" is used in the same breath.

I'm sure you have all heard the term, and many of you will know exactly what it means. I hope I'm not appearing to tell you how to suck eggs, but the following is an explanation of negative gearing written for someone who has no idea what it is. We start at the basics and build the concept brick by brick.

## Gearing

Gearing simply means borrowing to invest. If you want to buy an investment property and don't happen to have the $500,000 just sitting in a bank account as "Available Balance", chances are you're going to need to borrow money.

In most cases, the banks will not lend you 100% of the cost, so you have to have some skin in the game by stumping up a deposit. Let's assume it is 10% of the purchase price. You buy a $500,000 property, put in $50,000 of your own cash, and borrow the rest.

The best way to think about gearing is to think about a bicycle gear and wheel.

The outside of the wheel is the part that moves the most and rolls along the road. As the person riding the bike, peddling like crazy, what are you actually doing? Are you moving this part of the wheel?

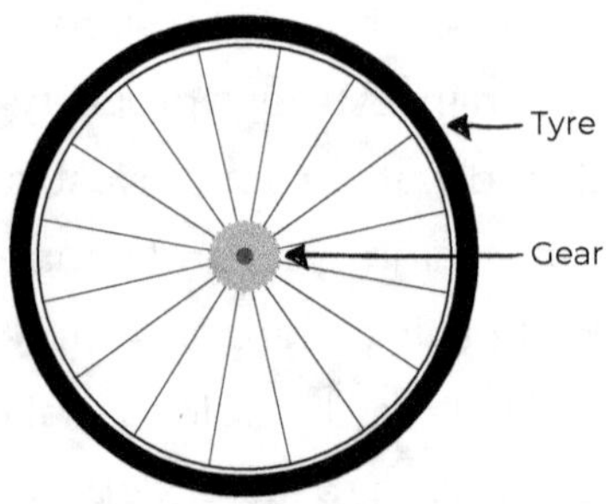

No. You are not moving the tyre. You are moving the gear – a much smaller part of the wheel. But this gear is part of the wheel, and when it moves, the rest of the wheel moves as well. So, by controlling the gear, you are controlling the whole wheel.

When applied to investing, the gear is your deposit, and the wheel is the investment property. You don't need $500,000 of your own cash to buy a $500,000 investment property. You could use as little as $50,000 of your own money and borrow the rest. This is all that gearing means. Using some of your own money to control an asset worth significantly more.

### *Technical Terms*

If you want to get really technical, using your own money to control an asset worth more is actually called "leveraging".

"Gearing" means borrowing money to invest.

Why would you do this? Because the value of a larger asset will increase more than a smaller asset.

Let's assume you have $50,000, and you want to invest it. You are considering putting it into a term deposit earning 5% per year, or using it as a deposit on a $500,000 investment property growing in value by 5% per year. Same rate of growth, but from a different starting point.

| Asset | Annual Growth | After 1 Year | After 2 Years | After 5 Years | After 10 Years | Total Gain |
|---|---|---|---|---|---|---|
| $50,000 Term Deposit | 5% | $52,500 | $55,125 | $63,814 | $81,444 | $31,444 |
| $500,000 Investment Property | 5% | $525,000 | $551,250 | $638,140 | $814,440 | $314,440 |

I know what you are thinking. Option A does not involve a $450,000 loan that interest is calculated on like Option B does. Option B also includes rates, insurances, management fees, maintenance, and the real possibility of bogan tenants who prioritise their Jim Beam over paying the rent.

And you are right. This is not a fair comparison, and it wasn't meant to be. This is merely a very simplistic explanation of what gearing means. Using a small asset to control a much larger one by borrowing money.

You probably did this when you bought your home. You put down a deposit and borrowed the rest. So, what's the difference?

Not all debt is created equal. Your home loan debt and your investment debt are treated very differently when it comes to paying your taxes.

## Good Debt vs Bad Debt

### Bad Debt

While you are living in your home, there is no taxation benefit from the loan. You can't claim any of the interest as a tax deduction, just as you can't claim the rates, insurances, and upkeep as a tax deduction.

## Good Debt

However, if the property is a rental that you are earning an income from, then there are quite a few tax deductions that you can and should be claiming, the main one being the interest on the loan.

## The Truth

This is why you often hear accountants using these terms – "good debt" and "bad debt".

I prefer to use the terms "bad debt" and "worse debt".

There's simply no such thing as good debt as far as I am concerned. Why pay a dollar in interest in order to save 30 cents in tax?

But when you have both bad debt and worse debt, it makes sense to focus on paying off the one that does not give you any taxation benefit before paying off the one that does.

In order to follow accepted naming conventions, I'll give up on my preferred terms and stick with the commonly used "good debt" vs "bad debt".

| Good Debt | Bad Debt |
|---|---|
| **You CAN claim the interest on these debts as a tax deduction** | **You CAN'T claim the interest on these debts as a tax deduction** |
| Your Investment Home Loan<br>Your Margin Loan<br>Your Business Loan<br>Your Business Car Lease<br>Your Business Credit Card | Your Home Loan<br>Your Personal Loan<br>Your Personal Car Loan<br>Your Personal Credit Card<br>Buy Now, Pay Later<br>Your HECS/HELP Debt<br>Your Tax Debt |

Gearing simply means borrowing to invest.

The money borrowed is typically good debt.

So, what are these three flavours of gearing we hear about – neutral, positive, and negative?

## Gearing: Neutral, Positive and Negative

Working out whether an investment is positively, neutrally, or negatively geared comes down to the balance of income and costs related to the property.

### Income and Costs

The income from an investment property is rent.

The costs of owning an investment property are:

- Interest on the investment loan.
- Council rates.
- Body corporate fees.
- Landlord insurance.
- Property management fees.
- Depreciation.
- General upkeep.

### Neutral Gearing

If the rent you are getting from the property perfectly equals the cost of holding it, your investment property is neutrally geared. It is not going to affect your overall taxable income from your job, because it is not increasing or decreasing it at all.

Cost of holding the property = rental income from tenants.

Rental income = $500 per week or $26,000 per year
Investment loan interest, council rates, insurances, management

fees, maintenance, and depreciation = $26,000 per year, or $500 per week
Income = $500
Costs = $500
Difference = $0

When the difference between the income and the costs is $0, the property is **neutrally geared.**

### Positive Gearing

If the rental income is higher than your holding costs, this is a fantastic result for you. You own a property that is hopefully going to increase in value over time, and it doesn't really cost you anything to own it. In fact, after paying all your expenses, you still have money left over.

This is positive gearing.

Rental income from tenants ≥ the cost of holding the property.

Rental income = $500 per week or $26,000 per year
Investment loan interest, council rates, insurances, management fees, maintenance, and depreciation = $20,800 per year, or $400 per week
Income = $500
Costs = $400
Difference = $100

You are making $100 per week on your investment property.

When the income is more than the costs, the property is **positively geared.**

All good news until the tax man finds out and wants his cut. You might be earning $70,000 a year in your job, and your employer has been withholding the right amount of tax from each payslip based on the assumption that you will earn $70,000 by the end of the financial year.

But once your positively geared investment property is taken into account, you actually earned $75,000 and have only paid tax on $70,000 of it. This will result in a tax bill.

## Negative Gearing

Negative gearing is where the holding costs of the property are more than the income you would get from it. You are losing money!

> Rental income from the tenant ≤ the cost of holding the property.

> Rental income = $500 per week or $26,000 per year
> Investment loan interest, council rates, insurances, management fees, maintenance, and depreciation = $31,200 per year, or $600 per week
> Income = $500
> Costs = $600
> Difference = -$100

When the income is less than the costs, the property is **negatively geared.**

Sounds like a crap investment, right?

At the end of the year, you've lost about $5,000 on the investment property, and this drops your taxable income down to $65,000. You've been paying tax on the assumption you are going to earn $70,000, so now the ATO has to refund you the extra tax that you paid through the year.

Sounding slightly better.

Now, the point I want to get to is that whether a property is positive, negative, or neutral, it doesn't really matter. What matters is that you can claim the interest as a tax deduction in all of those scenarios. If you had a positively geared property and suddenly weren't able to claim the interest as a tax deduction, then the property would be even more positively geared, and you'd pay more tax.

If your property was negatively geared and you didn't have a loan that you could claim as a tax deduction, then you would not be able to reduce the tax that you pay.

As weird as this sounds, this means that the loan for your investment property is actually a good debt. You can claim the interest as a tax deduction, which is impossible on the loan for your principal place of residence, which is why accountants often refer to that as bad debt.

If you have both debts – a loan against the house you are living in and a loan for your investment property – then you have both good and bad debt. In this case, most accountants would suggest you focus your energies on the bad debt and don't pay a single cent off the good debt. Paying off the investment loan will mean that you are actively reducing the tax-deductible interest.

Any spare coin that you have should be used to pay down the loan that has no taxation benefits – the home loan.

Let's get into some real examples. First, we need a crash course on how much tax you pay.

CHAPTER SIXTEEN

# Australian Income Tax

We have what's called a progressive tax schedule in Australia. The more you earn, the more tax you pay. We also have a range of tax brackets and thresholds. Once you go over a threshold and into a new tax bracket, you pay more tax. Here is a really simple snapshot of the tax brackets.

| Taxable Income | Tax Rate |
|---|---|
| 0–$18,200 | 0% |
| $18,201–$45,000 | 16% |
| $45,001–$135,000 | 30% |
| $135,001–$190,000 | 37% |
| $190,001 and over | 45% |

One very common misconception is that your tax rate is applied to all of your income, so someone earning $140,000 per year pays 37% of their income to the tax office. This is wrong and would be ridiculously unfair. Instead, you progress through all the tax brackets.

People earning under $18,200 per year pay no tax. This is called the tax-free threshold. Imagine you were earning $18,000 a year and paying no tax, and then your boss offered you a pay rise so you would be getting $20,000 per year. This puts you in the next tax bracket, and as some people believe, this means you will have to pay 16% of your income in tax. This would add up to $3,200, so out of your $20,000, you would end up with $16,800.

You would be better off not taking the pay rise, as your take-home cash each year would drop by $1,400.

Thankfully, this is not how tax is calculated.

In this example, you pay no tax on the first $18,200 you earn.

Then you pay 16% tax on any income above that.

So, on a $20,000 income, you pay no tax on the first $18,200, and then pay 16% on the remaining $1,800.

$$\$1,800 \times 16\% = \$288.$$

Your total tax is only $288 for the year, way better than the $3,200 some people think they have to pay.

This is why our tax schedule is progressive. You progress through each of the brackets and pay the appropriate tax for each one.

The guy earning $140,000 per year doesn't pay 37% tax on ALL of his income, even though he is in the 37% tax bracket.

He pays no tax on the first $18,200 he earns.

Then he pays 16% on the next $26,800.

Then he pays 30% on the next $90,000.

And finally, he pays 37% on the remaining $5,000.

| Taxable Income | Tax Rate | Taxable Amount | Tax Payable |
|---|---|---|---|
| 0–$18,200 | 0% | $18,200 | $0 |
| $18,201–$45,000 | 16% | $26,800 | $4,288 |
| $45,001–$135,000 | 30% | $90,000 | $27,000 |
| $135,001–$140,000 | 37% | $5,000 | $1,850 |
| Total | | $140,000 | $33,138 |

Therefore, he has to pay $33,138 tax.

As a percentage, that works out to be about 23.7% of his total income. Way better than the 37% he assumed he was paying.

If you are an employee, then all this is looked after for you by the employer. They automatically deduct your income tax from your salary each fortnight, and they pay it to the tax office on your behalf, so you don't have to worry about it.

If your income is fairly stable, then you'll have paid your correct tax as you go, and when you lodge your tax return, you won't get a bill or a refund. If you claimed some deductions like laundry, then this amount can be taken off your taxable income.

Let's say Phil has $500 worth of laundry expenses for the year. His employer has been withholding the right amount of tax from his payslip on the assumption he earns $140,000 over the year. However, when we subtract his laundry expenses, his taxable income is $139,500, not the $140,000 he has paid tax on.

In this scenario, he has paid too much tax and now needs to get some of it back.

**AUSTRALIAN INCOME TAX**

| Taxable Income | Tax Rate | Taxable Amount | Tax Payable |
|---|---|---|---|
| 0–$18,200 | 0% | $18,200 | $0 |
| $18,201–$45,000 | 16% | $26,800 | $4,288 |
| $45,001–$135,000 | 30% | $90,000 | $27,000 |
| $135,001–$139,500 | 37% | $4,500 | $1,665 |
| Total | | $139,500 | $32,953 |

Woohoo! He now gets a cheque for $185 as a refund from the tax office.

You with me? Okay, let's see what happens to Phil's tax when he buys an investment property.

**Phil buys a neutrally geared investment property.**

Rent = $500 per week

Costs = $500 per week

Phil's taxable income from his job = $140,000

Phil's adjusted taxable income after allowing for his investment = $140,000

His investment property neither made nor lost money. It's neutral, so it has no impact on Phil's income tax. He doesn't get a tax bill or a refund.

**Phil buys a positively geared investment property.**

Rent = $500 per week

Costs = $400 per week

Total investment profit for the year = $5,200

Phil's taxable income from his job = $140,000

Phil's adjusted taxable income after allowing for his investment: $145,200

His investment property made money, and this profit gets added to his taxable income. His employer couldn't care less about his investment so deducts his tax based on the assumption he is going to earn his contracted salary of $140,000. But in reality, Phil has earned $145,200 over the year and only paid tax on $140,000 of it.

He now has to pay more tax on the extra $5,200.

| Taxable Income | Tax Rate | Taxable Amount | Tax Payable |
|---|---|---|---|
| 0–$18,200 | 0% | $18,200 | $0 |
| $18,201–$45,000 | 16% | $26,800 | $4,288 |
| $45,001–$135,000 | 30% | $90,000 | $27,000 |
| $135,001–$145,200 | 37% | $10,200 | $3,774 |
| Total | | $145,200 | $35,062 |

His employer has paid $33,138, which means Phil is short $1,924.

No tax refund for Phil this year. In fact, he gets a bill for $1,924 that he has to pay to the tax office.

**Phil buys a negatively geared investment property.**
Rent = $500 per week
Costs = $600 per week

Phil is losing money here. He has had to chip in an extra $5,200 of his own money over the year, as the rental income alone was not enough to cover all the costs. The good thing here is that Phil can subtract that amount from his taxable income.

Total investment loss for the year = $5,200
Phil's taxable income from his job = $140,000

Phil's adjusted taxable income after allowing for his investment = $134,800

His investment property lost money, and this loss gets subtracted from his taxable income. His employer has been withholding his tax based on the assumption he is going to earn his contracted salary of $140,000. But in reality, Phil has only earned $134,800 so has paid too much tax.

He should now get a refund on the extra tax he has paid.

| Taxable Income | Tax Rate | Taxable Amount | Tax Payable |
|---|---|---|---|
| 0–$18,200 | 0% | $18,200 | $0 |
| $18,201–$45,000 | 16% | $26,800 | $4,288 |
| $45,001–$134,800 | 30% | $89,800 | $26,940 |
| Total | | $134,800 | $31,228 |

His employer has paid $33,138, but Phil is only required to pay $31,228, so Phil gets a refund of $1,910.

Still sounds crap, though, right? Phil effectively lost $5,200 on the property in that year and then got back $1,910 in his tax return. That's still $3,290 short of breaking even.

Even with the tax deductions, Phil is down almost $3,300 for the year on his investment.

And this is what a lot of people don't see. They hate paying tax, so when an opportunity comes along that allows them to pay less tax, it grabs their attention.

It's like paying $1 in interest in order to save 30 cents in tax.

Why would anyone do it?

The main reason is that most investors are going for the capital gain, and the tax deductions are just the cream on the cake.

Phil is down $3,290 over the year after tax. If his $500k property increases in value by just 1% during the year, it will have gone up by $5,000, more than covering the after-tax loss. Of course, Phil will only realise this gain when he sells the property, and as we discussed above, he'll have to contend with the associated costs such as real estate commission and CGT.

CHAPTER SEVENTEEN

# Investment Property Deductions

So far, we have only talked about the "holding costs" of an investment property and how that relates to positive and negative gearing, but what exactly are these costs?

## Disclaimer Time

You guessed it. I'm not an accountant. I cannot give you any advice about your taxes, and anything I write here should not be considered advice. If you buy an investment property, talk to an accountant. All I will do is help you get the loan.

The following section looks at the deductions that I think I would be allowed to claim if I bought an investment property. It's got nothing to do with you! Just sayin'.

## Costs When Purchasing

When buying a property, there are quite a few things you need to pay for aside from just the deposit. Most of these are not tax-deductible themselves, but the interest paid on them usually is. Let's run through the likely suspects.

## Stamp Duty/Land Tax

Stamp duty is a standover tax that Al Capone could have only dreamt about.

Like a Hollywood mafia movie where enforcers intimidate shopkeepers to pay them protection money, the Australian states levy a similar tax on people buying property. They see Jim buying a property from Jane and then muscle their way into the transaction happening on their turf.

"We'll take a cut of that," they say.

Stamp duty is calculated as a percentage of the purchase price and differs across states and territories. It is also based on whether it is for the purchase of the buyer's first home, a home that they will live in but not their first, or an investment property.

It can be quite a large expense, and for people who have just enough deposit to put down, it can chew up so much of their savings that they don't have enough left to make the purchase possible.

Some states are moving toward a land tax alternative, where instead of the big one-off lump-sum payment at settlement, stamp duty is replaced by a much smaller tax payable each year that the property is owned.

If you really hate stamp duty, consider a move across the ditch, where Kiwis pay NO stamp duty!

## Land Transfer Registration Fee

When you buy a property, fork out tens of thousands of dollars on the deposit and stamp duty, and take on a mortgage of hundreds of thousands of dollars, it would pay to make sure you are definitely the owner of the property. This is where the land transfer registration comes to reassure you. At a cost, of course.

When a property is transferred into your name, the database at the relevant state Land Registry office is updated to show you are the new owner. The costs vary across states and territories, but they all have something fairly similar to each other.

My gripe is that they call this a fee, but in reality, it is a tax or a levy, as the amount you pay is based on the value of the property. Does registering the new owner of a property in the database really take more time and labour if the value of the property is higher?

## Mortgage Registration Fees

Now, this one is a fee, as it is the same for everyone and every property.

If you needed a loan to buy the property, the bank will place a mortgage over the property to basically say they pretty much own it until you repay the debt. This also needs to be registered with the government, and they will sting you a couple of hundred dollars to deregister the previous bank, and another couple of hundred to register the new one.

## Pest and Building Report

Would you want to know if the property you are buying has active white ants? Would you want to know if there aren't any at the moment, but there is visible damage from previous infestations?

The new tiling in the bathroom that the sellers completed just before listing the property looks amazing. But is it covering up a wall of damp mildew and mould?

Is the pool and fence certified?

Did the owners get council approval for the granny flat?

Why is that power point upside down?

Forking out between $500 and $1,000 for a good pest and building inspection before you buy a property is easily the best investment you can possibly make. Not only will a good inspector find the issues the agent failed to bring to your attention, having a report can also save your backside when you need to make a building insurance claim years later.

### Conveyancing Solicitor

A good conveyancing solicitor will make the transfer of ownership from the seller to you as smooth as possible. Their job is to:

- Go over the contract and add any special clauses they think might protect you.
- Complete searches on the property to make sure the rates are paid, it's not going to get flooded every summer, and that there aren't any plans to build a highway through the middle of it.
- Represent you at the settlement, ensuring the right people are paid the right amount of money.
- Ensure ownership is transferred into your name and your stamp duty is paid.

### Lender Set-Up Fees

Most banks will have some fees that are taken out of the loan amount at settlement. These could include any of the following:

- Application fee.
- Annual fee in advance.
- Valuation fee.
- Legal fees for the bank's solicitor to draw up the loan contracts.
- Settlement fee (PEXA).
- Title search fee.
- Lenders mortgage insurance.

These will all be outlined in the loan contract that you sign before settlement.

## Depreciation

Now, this is a case of the tax office being really generous. I couldn't count the number of times I have tried to explain depreciation to a first-time investor only for them to shake their head and assume I'm pulling their leg. But I shit you not.

An investment property is made up of the land, the building, and the fittings and fixtures attached to the building, like ovens, stoves, curtains, light fittings, carpets, hot water systems, etc.

If you are familiar with children, you will know that everything they touch turns to crap very quickly. Even without children ruining everything in a house, eventually the stove, curtains, dishwasher, and hot water system will come to the end of their useful lives and will need to be replaced. As the landlord, you are responsible for replacing these for the tenants very quickly after they break.

Thankfully, you can claim the cost of these as a tax deduction. You may not be able to claim the whole cost in the financial year that you purchased them, but you can instead claim 20% of the cost each year for the next five years.

Sounds reasonable, yeah?

Well, get this. You can also claim the cost of the house. The ATO allows you to claim 2.5% of the cost of the building itself every year for 40 years. Say you built a house for $400,000, you could claim $10,000 per year as a deduction for the next 40 years.

HUGE caveats here! Rules around depreciation have changed significantly over time, and my explanation is about as robust as a politician's tweet. Assume nothing when it comes to buying an investment property. You don't want to buy a property expecting to claim significant depreciation only to find out there is none. A depreciation schedule completed by a quantity surveyor will tell you exactly how much you can claim.

***BEWARE!***

Don't buy a property BECAUSE of depreciation.

Too many people chase the tax deductions when the real goal is capital growth. Buying a brand-new property so you can claim the maximum tax deductions could see you paying significantly more than a better-priced older home in a superior location. You can also create depreciation in older properties by renovating.

Depreciation is a nice little cherry on top of the cake, but that's it. It shouldn't be the reason you buy the cake. With that in mind, I'm leaving it out of my example calculations.

## Example Property Purchase

How do all the above add up, and what does it look like in a real example? Let's look at an investment property purchase in Queensland. We will assume that the buyers have equity in another property that they can use for the deposit.

| Purchase Price | $700,000.00 |
|---|---|
| **State Fees and Charges** | |
| Qld Stamp Duty | $24,525.00 |
| Land Title Registration Fee | $2,563.00 |
| Mortgage Registration Fee | $238.00 |
| **Lender Costs** | |
| Application Fee | $600.00 |
| Title Search Fee | $23.27 |
| PEXA Settlement Fee | $123.97 |
| **Sundries** | |
| Conveyancing Costs | $1,800.00 |
| Pest and Building Report | $750.00 |
| **Total** | $30,623.24 |

## Tax Deductibility

All of the above costs are incurred during the purchase of the property and are therefore not deductible as a rule (obviously, check with your accountant). But is there a way to at least get some sort of tax break for these?

## Borrowing the Costs

The stamp duty may not be tax-deductible, but the interest on the loan is. So instead of stumping up the stamp duty from cash that could be used to reduce non-tax-effective debt, many investors simply borrow it. The same goes for all the other costs in the above table.

Buying a $700,000 investment property will actually cost you around $730,000. If the investor borrows the entire $730,000, they should be able to claim the interest on the entire debt as a tax deduction.

But who is going to lend someone $730,000 and take a property worth less than the loan as security?

No one.

## Splitting the Loan

If you have another property that has equity in it, you can borrow against that property as well as the property being purchased. But beware of cross-collateralisation. This is where the bank takes both properties as security for both loans, and 100% of the time, this benefits the bank more than the borrower. There really is no need for it, and a simpler option is to split the loans according to their purpose and secure them to the separate properties.

The easiest way to demonstrate this is with an example.

Bob's home is worth $750,000, and his loan is down to $400,000, so he has $350,000 in equity.

He wants to purchase an investment property for $700,000. As we know, this will actually cost him about $730,000 once the associated costs are taken into account. Ideally, he doesn't want to borrow more than 80% of the value of the new property, as that will incur lenders mortgage insurance.

$$\$700{,}000 \times 80\% = \$560{,}000$$

The investment property will have a loan of $560,000 against it, which means Bob still has to come up with the remaining $170,000.

He can borrow this against his owner-occupied home. He already has a $400,000 loan, and if he increases this to $570,000, he will have the funds to pay the difference between the purchase cost and the 80% investment loan. This loan should also be split, as $400,000 of it is not tax-deductible, and $170,000 of it is.

Bob ends up with three loans:

1. $400,000 original home loan secured by his owner-occupied home.
2. $170,000 investment loan used for the 20% deposit plus costs for the investment purchase, but secured by his owner-occupied home.
3. $560,000 investment loan secured by new investment property.

This avoids lenders mortgage insurance and cross-collateralisation while keeping the loans separated for their different purposes, which will keep his accountant happy.

He has also borrowed 100% of the purchase price plus the associated costs, and the interest on that combined debt will be tax-deductible.

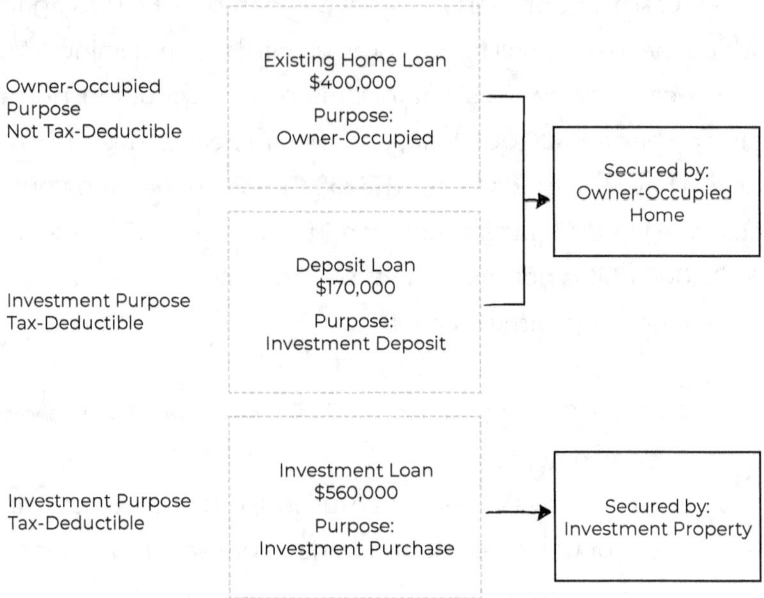


Before we delve into the tax calculations, let's have a quick look at how your investment property cash flow can help you pay off your owner-occupied home loan faster.

## Cash Flow

Move your money around in a way that benefits you.

If you have made it this far, then you know the following:

- The loan for the property we live in is bad debt. The interest cannot be claimed as a tax deduction. It makes sense to focus our energy on paying this mongrel off as quickly as possible.
- Interest on the home loan is calculated daily, so the sooner we reduce the balance of the loan, the less interest we pay.

- An offset account allows you to reduce the effective balance that interest is calculated on in the home loan the minute you get paid.
- The interest we pay on the home loan reduces when we have more money in the offset account for longer.

I know most of you are well ahead of me here and can see where this is going.

How should Bob structure his cash flow once he buys an investment property?

### Bob's Original Cash Flow

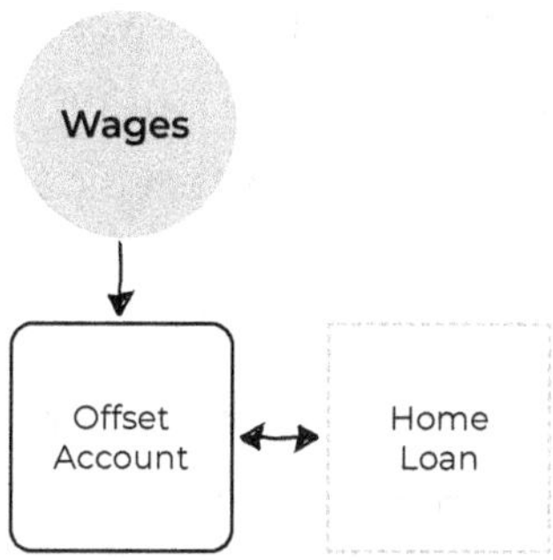


Bob's income goes straight into his offset account. The longer it stays in his account, the less interest he pays on the home loan.

### Bob's New Cash Flow

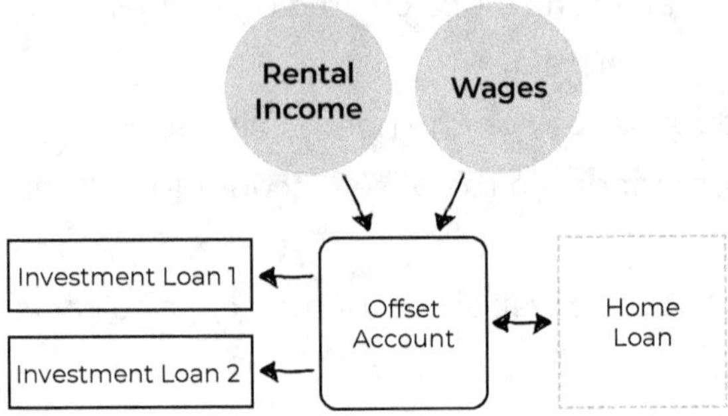


Pretty simple, huh? Bob simply gets the property manager to deposit the rent into his offset account, and this keeps even more money in his offset account until the investment loan repayment and other investment costs come out. While it is in there, it is reducing the balance that interest is calculated on in his home loan – AKA bad debt.

But is this as smart as it looks?

Bob now has all the investment property income and all the investment costs like rates and insurances flowing through his personal account. This isn't a huge issue, but when it comes to tax time and he has to work out his total investment income and costs for the year, having everything go through the one account could be messy and difficult to track.

## Bob's New (and Improved) Cash Flow

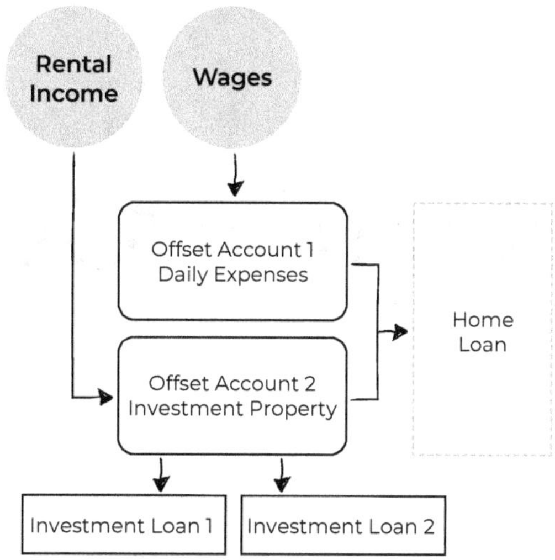


Now Bob has two offset accounts, and the combined balance of these is coming off his home loan.

He is also running separate accounts for his personal expenses and his investment property. He has an account that is dedicated to his investment property. Rent goes into this account, and all associated expenses come out of it. At the end of the financial year, his bookkeeping is a breeze.

## CHAPTER EIGHTEEN

# Interest Rates

Before 2014, the only difference between a home loan and an investment loan was the spelling. With most banks, the rates, fees, and loan features were all the same, and the difference was in name only. Even the repayment type made no difference to the rate that you got.

But due to a boom in investment lending, the banking regulator got the heebie-jeebies and decided that the banks needed to slow down giving loans to investors, so it imposed limits on how much they could lend. Banks were then forced into a situation where they had to discourage borrowers from applying for investment loans.

How on earth were they going to do that? Would they use the finance equivalent of a bouncer and simply let the first best-dressed people in and then close the doors once their limit was reached? Or would they get more picky and only let the beautiful people in – those with designer brand clothes, lots of hair product, and fat wallets?

This would be the Bob Hope school of thought, as he once

famously said, "A bank is a place that will lend you money if you can prove that you don't need it."

Alas, our fine Australian banks did nothing of the sort. Instead, they simply raised the interest rates on investment loans. In a million years, who would have ever thought the banks would take this regulatory decision to slow down investment lending as an opportunity to increase profits?

As surprising as it isn't, that is what they did. They jacked up rates on investment loans, which certainly did discourage some potential investors, and they made money while doing it.

They also increased the rates further on investment loans, which had interest-only repayments, which was a real stroke of brilliance considering most investment loans were interest-only.

But I digress. The whole point of this section is to tell you that with most banks, the interest rate you get is based on the loan and repayment type, with owner-occupied principal and interest loans as the cheapest, and investment interest-only loans as the most expensive.

For the upcoming calculations, I'm going to assume the following rates, which are just examples:

| Loan Type | Repayment Type | Interest Rate |
|---|---|---|
| Owner-Occupied | Principal and Interest | 6.00% |
| | Interest Only | 6.25% |
| Investment | Principal and Interest | 6.50% |
| | Interest Only | 6.75% |

## Interest Only

If you thought the debt-reduction strategy of going into more debt was absurd, well, buckle up. I'm going to do my best to explain why many people not only go into more debt as a way of becoming debt-free, but also do so with no intention of paying the loan off.

It all comes back to good debt vs bad debt. If you have both, then most accountants would recommend you pay the minimum on the good debts so that every spare dollar is getting paid off the bad debt.

And as it is only the interest on the investment loan that is tax-deductible (not the principal), many investors just pay that. This means the investment loan doesn't actually reduce. The balance of the loan remains the same as long as it is set to interest-only (IO) payments.

The other major drawback with IO payments is the fact the interest rate is often a fair whack higher than the principal and interest (P&I) rate. For our calculations, we will assume the rates in the table above.

## How does paying P&I or IO affect Bob?

### Scenario 1 – Bob makes P&I payments on all loans.

| Loan | Balance | Interest Rate | Loan Term | Monthly Interest | Monthly Repayment |
|---|---|---|---|---|---|
| Home Loan | $400,000 | 6.00% | 30 Years | $2,000 | $2,398 |

| Loan | Balance | Interest Rate | Loan Term | Monthly Interest | Monthly Repayment |
|---|---|---|---|---|---|
| Investment Loan 1 | $170,000 | 6.50% | 30 Years | $921 | $1,075 |
| Investment Loan 2 | $560,000 | 6.50% | 30 Years | $3,033 | $3,540 |
| Total | $730,000 | | | $3,954 | **$4,615** |

Bob is making a total monthly repayment on the investment loans of $4,615, but only $3,954 of that is interest and therefore deductible. He's making a $661 payment off his investment loans each month, which is really doing nothing except reducing his good debt and therefore tax-deductible interest in future months.

Most accountants would recommend he instead pay that $661 per month off his bad debt. To do this, he would need to change his repayment on the investment loans to interest only, and this means higher interest rates on those loans.

### Scenario 2 – Bob makes P&I payments on his home loan, and IO payments on the investment loans.

| Loan | Balance | Interest Rate | Loan Term | Monthly Interest | Monthly Repayment |
|---|---|---|---|---|---|
| Home Loan | $400,000 | 6.00% | 30 Years | $2,000 | $2,398 |

| Loan | Balance | Interest Rate | Loan Term | Monthly Interest |
|---|---|---|---|---|
| Investment Loan 1 | $170,000 | 6.75% | 30 Years | $956 |
| Investment Loan 2 | $560,000 | 6.75% | 30 Years | $3,150 |
| Total | $730,000 | | | $4,106 |

This has reduced his payments to the investment loans from $4,615 to $4,106 per month – a difference of $509.

If Bob paid that $509 per month off his home loan instead of the investment loans, he would cut 10.5 years off the term of the loan and save nearly $185,000 in the process.

In reality, banks will usually only allow a loan to have interest-only payments for five years at a time. After that time, it will revert to P&I payments, and this could be higher than if it had been P&I from the start, as it now has to be repaid in the remaining 25 years, rather than the original 30 years.

It is possible to refinance the loan after the initial five-year interest-only period has finished in order to get another five years, which is the only way that Bob would be able to achieve the results above.

## Stitching It All Together

The three ways that buying an investment property can help reduce debt are capital growth, tax deductions, and cash flow.

And here is the broken record again.

Buying an investment property is not for everyone. Whether you make money on it depends on so many different variables, most of which are out of your control. And this is why it is vital to do your research and know the maths before you take the plunge.

In my opinion, you simply MUST consult an accountant before you become an investor to make sure the numbers stack up. Below is an example of a realistic scenario that I run for my investor clients, which they then get verified by their accountants.

I am not going to go into a granular level of detail, as that would be an entire book in itself. Instead, I will lay out the variables, assume they are constant over time (they never are), and provide the projections.

## Investor

| Name | Bob |
|---|---|
| Employment | High School Teacher |
| Salary | $110,000 per year |
| Tax | $23,788 per year |
| Home Value | $750,000 |
| Home Loan | $400,000 |
| Interest Rate | 6.00% |
| P&I Repayment | $2,398 |
| Term Remaining | 30 Years |

## Investment Property

The example investment property I am going to use is an existing house that does not include any depreciation at all.

| Purchase Price | $700,000 |
|---|---|
| Stamp Duty (Qld) | $24,525 |
| Transfer of Title | $2,563 |
| Mortgage Registration Fee | $238 |
| Conveyancing Costs | $1,800 |
| Pest and Building Costs | $750 |
| Loan Application Fee | $600 |
| Title Search Fee | $23 |
| PEXA Settlement Fee | $124 |
| Total Purchase Cost | $730,623 |

## Income and Expenses

| | |
|---|---|
| **Rental Income Weekly** | $650 |
| **Rental Income Annually** | $33,800 |
| | |
| **Property Management** | $2,733 |
| **Letting Fees** | $650 |
| **Council Rates** | $2,500 |
| **Landlord Insurance** | $1,250 |
| **Maintenance** | $1,000 |
| **Total Annual Expenses** | $8,133 |

## Loan Structure

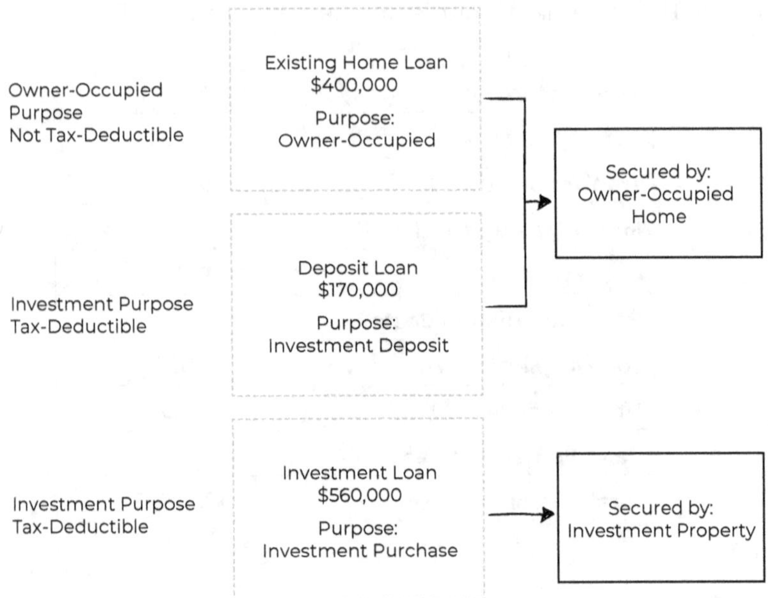

## Investment Loans

Bob will be paying IO for the first five years on his investment loans, so he can funnel any spare cash into his home loan. After this, the repayments will revert to P&I for the remaining 25 years.

| Loan | Balance | Interest Rate | Monthly Interest (First 5 Years) | P&I Payment (Remaining 25 Years) |
|---|---|---|---|---|
| Deposit Loan | $170,000 | 6.75% | $956 | $1,175 |
| Main Loan | $560,000 | 6.75% | $3,150 | $3,869 |
| **Totals** | **$730,000** | | **$4,106** | **$5,044** |
| **Annual Totals** | | | **$49,272** | **$60,528** |

For the first five years, Bob will be paying $49,272 interest per year to cover the two investment loans.

After five years, this will increase to $60,528 per year when the repayment changes from IO to P&I.

## Cash Flow

Annual Income: $33,800

Annual Interest: $49,272

Annual Expenses: $8,133

Annual Loss: $23,605

Bob is losing money here. Big time!

He is in the hole $23,605, which is close to a quarter of his income. This property isn't just negatively geared, it is **NEGATIVELY** geared.

### Tax Implications

Bob earns $110,000 per year, which attracts $23,788 a year in tax. His employer withholds this for him, so at the end of the financial year, he has no tax bill, and his tax return is fairly minimal.

PAYG Income: $110,000
minus
Investment Loss: $23,605
equals
New Taxable Income: $86,395

Once we factor in the loss on the investment property, Bob's income has gone from $110,000 to $86,395.

As he has already paid $23,788 in tax that has been automatically deducted from his payslips each fortnight, he has effectively paid more tax than he should have.

Annual tax on income of $86,395 = $16,706
Tax Refund coming to Bob = $7,081

Bob paid $23,788 in tax in the financial year on the assumption he was going to earn $110,000 in taxable income. The reality is that his taxable income reduced to $86,395 for the year, and the tax on that is only $16,706, so Bob has overpaid his taxes through the year.

He should now be eligible for a tax return of the difference, which is $7,081.

Bob's investment cost him $23,605, but he got $7,081 of this back in his tax return. Still a shit deal, right? I mean, even after getting his tax return, Bob still lost $16,524.

Pre-tax Loss = $23,605

Post-tax Loss = $16,524

## Challenges

The biggest challenge that people like Bob face is cash flow. The rent is not covering the cost of owning the property, so Bob has to stump up the difference throughout the year; $23,605 is almost $2,000 per month that he has to fork out in order to call himself a landlord. This is on top of his home loan and living expenses.

For most people, they simply do not have a spare $2,000 per month to make this workable, and this is without factoring in things that could go wrong, like the property sitting vacant or the tenants not paying the rent.

At the end of the financial year, Bob gets his return of $7,081, but he has to wear that pre-tax loss in the 12 months before doing his taxes.

Even after getting his tax return, his investment still cost him $16,524 for the year, which is $1,377 per month, or $318 per week.

## Silver Lining

Most people looking at this scenario would dismiss it as a bad investment. But plenty of people like Bob proceed with exactly this kind of purchase, some with even worse cash flow. Why?

1. Forced Savings

   In general, Australians will cut back on every other expense before they stop paying bank loans. A purchase like this might force Bob to put that $318 a week away into an investment that doesn't allow him to get it back out again whenever he wants.

2. Capital Growth

   His after-tax loss of $16,524 works out to be just under 2.4% of the value of the property. If the investment property increases in value by more than this each year, then he will come out ahead when he eventually sells the property. But don't forget that real estate commissions and capital gains tax need to be accounted for here as well.

3. Cash Flow Improvements

   Over time, Bob should find it easier to service this investment for a few reasons:

   - The loan balance will not increase. In fact, it will eventually start to decrease.
   - His wages should increase. (But so will the cost of everything else.)
   - The rent he receives should also increase. (But so will the property expenses.)

   If we assume both his income and his living expenses increase in line with inflation of, say, 3% per year, then they cancel each other out.

## SUMMARY

Oh man, do you really need more words from me?

If I haven't confused the hell out of you over the last 20 pages or so, then at least one of us deserves a pat on the back.

Buying an investment property is complicated and involves a lot of maths. If you aren't 100% confident your sums are correct, you need a maths tutor called an accountant who can run the projections, so you know what you are getting yourself into.

## CHAPTER NINETEEN

# Reduce Debt or Buy Shares

Being a landlord can accelerate your debt-reduction goals, but it can also suck. Big time. This section is for those of you who might want to invest before you have completely paid off your loan, just not in property.

**HACK #11**

*Debt Recycling.*

For most people, this is the share market, and though there are other options, it's investing in shares that I am going to use as an example for no better reason than I'm lazy.

So that I don't sound like I'm giving advice, I'm just going to tell you about a mate of mine – Jim.

Jim's aunty made a mountain of money from multi-level marketing, working from home at hours that suited her (cough, bullshit, cough). She left Jim a handy $10k in her will.

Jim's not sure what to do. He'd like to use it to pay down his mortgage but is also thinking about using it to buy shares.

Many people are confused when it comes to debt reduction vs wealth creation. They want to pay off their owner-occupied debt as the interest payable is not tax-deductible and therefore it is best retired as quickly as possible. However, they may also be attracted to buying a slice of their favourite company before achieving their goal of becoming debt-free.

Most people look at this scenario as an either/or equation. We **either** reduce our debt **or** buy shares.

What would you do if you were Jim? Pay down the debt? Buy shares? A bit of both?

Let's say Jim has $100,000 of owner-occupied debt. The interest he pays on this loan is not tax-deductible, so we usually call this "bad debt". It makes sense to smash this debt and get rid of it as quickly as possible. Alternatively, if Jim had a $100,000 loan that he had used to buy an investment property or a share portfolio, then that is investment debt and the interest can be used as a tax deduction, so we call this "good debt".

If Jim has some good debt and also some bad debt, then most accountants would suggest that he focus on getting rid of the bad debt first, as it offers no taxation benefit. For this reason, we would usually set up Jim's bad debt to have principal and interest repayments, while on the good debt, he'd just pay the interest. This will allow him to focus any and all spare funds on hammering that bad debt.

So, debt reduction typically looks like this:

## Option 1 – Jim decides against buying shares and instead uses the $10k to pay down his debt.

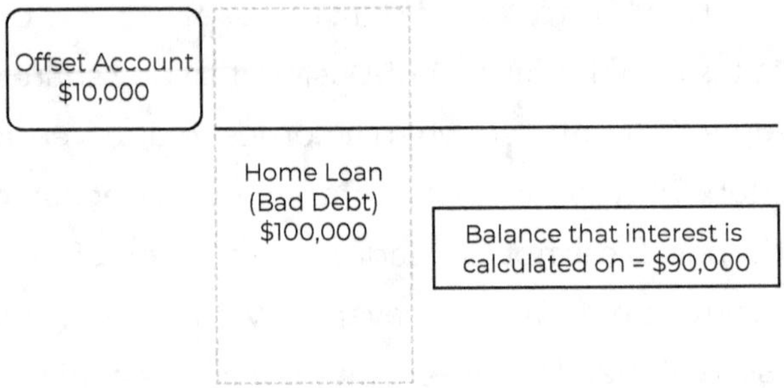


Jim is a smart cookie and has always used an offset account, so if he keeps the funds in the offset account, he's only paying interest on $90k worth of debt. It's the same as transferring the funds directly into the loan in terms of how much interest is calculated. The more money he saves in the offset account, the less interest he pays on the home loan.

Some people prefer to put the money into the home loan. In the offset account, it's just a bit too easy to access and spend on stuff that they don't really need. So, they build up their offset balance, then transfer the funds into the home loan so it is a little more "out of sight, out of mind".

So, if Jim was worried about having ATM access to his $10,000, then he might do the following:

### Transfer Offset Funds to Home Loan

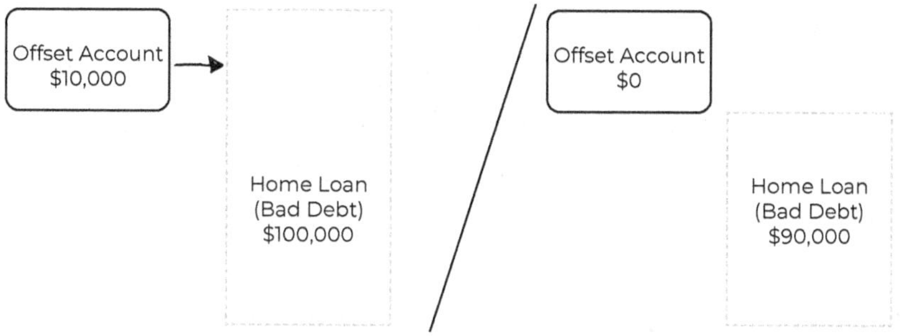


He transfers the money into the home loan. This reduces the offset balance to $0, but the home loan is also down to $90k. Mathematically – same, same.

In both scenarios, Jim is only paying interest on $90k.

Jim gets this, and he loves to see his debt reduce, but with the low interest rates and all his mates jumping on the ASX bandwagon, he's also keen to dip his toe in the water and start investing for long-term wealth creation, but he doesn't want to wait until the $100,000 bad debt is completely paid out before he starts investing. Most people would do this in a way that doesn't make the most sense taxation-wise.

## Option 2 – Jim uses the $10k to buy shares and puts his debt-reduction goal on ice.

Some people in Jim's shoes would take the $10,000 from the offset account and use it to buy shares. Now they have $0 in the offset account, the home loan is fully drawn at $100k, but they do have $10k worth of shares.

Before they bought the shares, they had $10,000 in the offset account, and this meant the bank could only calculate interest on

$90,000 in the home loan. Now they have used that $10,000, the balance that interest is calculated on in the home loan is back at $100,000, none of which is tax-deductible.

What if there was a way to still have $100k of debt and $10k of shares, but also get a little tax deduction?

Jim talks to his accountant, financial advisor, mortgage broker, baker, postman, and footy coach about another way of doing it.

## Option 3 – Reduce bad debt, split loan, use redraw to buy shares.

Jim decides that a better way to do it would be to use that $10,000 in the offset account to pay down the home loan to $90,000. This would give him $10,000 in redraw on the loan. He then splits that off into a separate loan account of $10,000 and uses that money to buy the shares.

### Step 1 – Use the $10k to pay down the home loan.

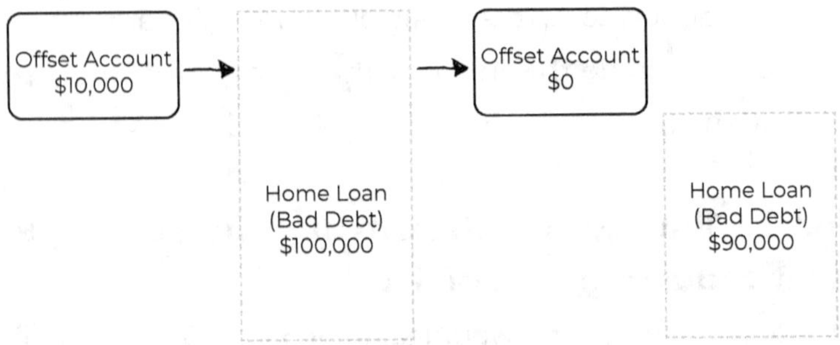


### Step 2 – Jim gets his mortgage broker to split the loan into two accounts. One for $90k and a new one for $10k.

The $10k loan is not drawn – the whole $10k is available. He then draws that $10k out and uses it to buy shares.

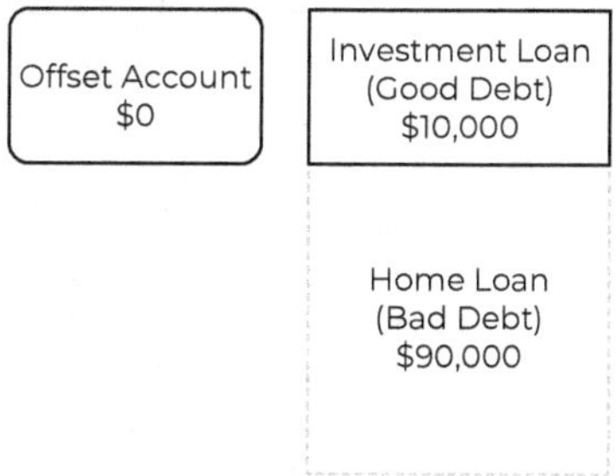


The overall position is exactly the same. He still has $100,000 worth of debt and $10,000 worth of shares. But the main difference now is that he can claim the interest on the $10,000 loan split as a tax deduction, as the purpose of that debt was to buy the shares. So now his bad debt is $90,000, and his good debt is $10,000. He's just recycled $10,000 worth of debt, turning it from bad debt to good debt.

**Step 3 – Build up offset account to $10,000 and repeat.**

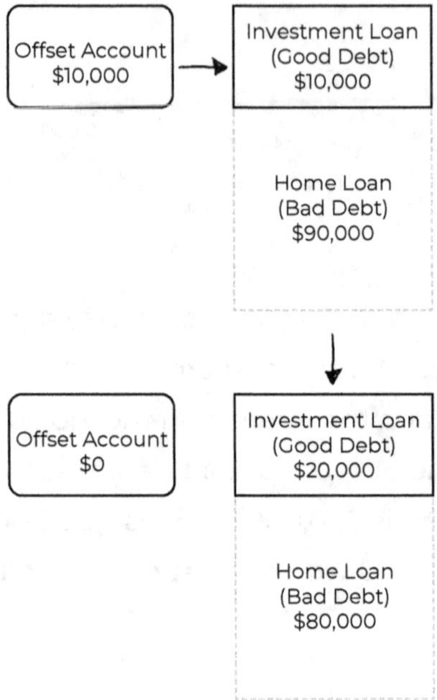


**Step 4 – Continue the process until all bad debt has been recycled into good debt.**

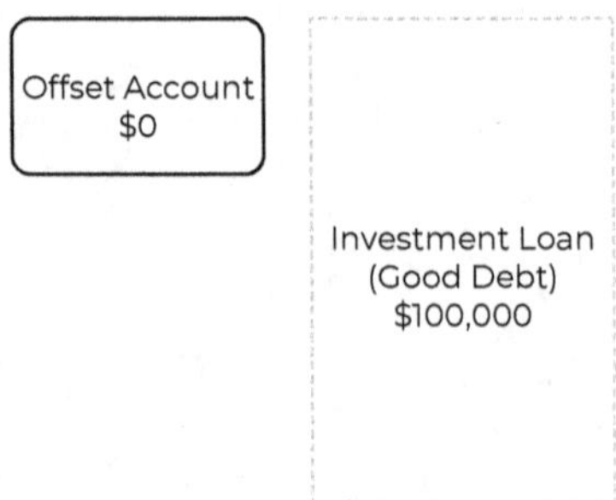

Debt recycling makes sense. Especially if:

- You already have a bad debt home loan.
- You have no interest in becoming a landlord.
- You are interested in the share market.
- You want to structure your accounts in a way that gives you tax benefits.

For a variety of reasons, debt recycling is an extremely difficult concept to grasp for some rusted-on people in finance. But at its core, it's actually very simple.

If you have bad debt and want to invest before becoming completely debt-free, simply structure it in a way that gives you a tax benefit.

That's it.

***BEWARE!***

Some banks get debt recycling. Some will ask if you need an interpreter when you ask about it.

If you want to look into your options here, you really should talk to a mortgage broker who knows debt recycling inside out and knows which banks are very good for recyclers.

Ideally, Jim would want to already be with the right lender before he puts his share market plan into action. When he goes to split his loan, for many banks, this could be a whole new application that takes over a month to complete.

Lenders that have a flexible and fast variation process are the ones Jim should be going for, as well as seeking a great interest rate and an offset account.

Not sure if I mentioned this already, so ...

I'm not a financial planner. This is not advice. This is just a story about my mate Jim and how he decided to recycle his debt from bad to good.

If you are thinking about replicating Jim's strategy, make sure you talk to your accountant, financial planner, mortgage broker, baker, postie, and footy coach.

CONCLUSION

# You're the Boss Now

If you've made it this far, well done. You now know more about home loans than the average borrower, and definitely more than that bloke on TikTok.

We've covered a lot in this book – how banks make their money, how loan structures really work, how small changes can save you tens (or even hundreds) of thousands of dollars, and how to use the bank's own products to your advantage. And we did it all without gimmicks, hype, or "one weird trick" clickbait. Just real, practical strategies that work.

Banks aren't in the business of helping you pay off your loan faster. They're in the business of making money from your loan for as long as possible. That's not evil. It's just how business works. But that doesn't mean you have to play by their default rules.

Now, you know how to play a smarter game.

You've learned:

- That the way interest is calculated matters.
- That structuring your loan the right way gives you flexibility, control, and speed.
- That mathematically, there's not a lot of difference between using an offset account or parking your savings in the loan itself as redraw. But there are huge tax implications for each scenario.
- That comparing loans based on interest rate alone is like choosing a car based only on colour.
- And that, yes, if you want to, you can take things further – into debt recycling and wealth-building territory.

But none of this knowledge matters if it stays trapped in your head.

So, here's what I want you to do next:

- Review your current loan. Is it set up to help you win, or help the bank win?
- Check your repayment frequency. Does it align with your income?
- Could you improve your cash flow by using an all-in-one loan or an offset package?
- Run the numbers. How much could you save by making small changes today?

And if you're not sure where to start, talk to a broker who actually understands strategy, not just product. Ask better questions and push for better answers.

Because now, you know what's possible.

This book wasn't written to scare you or sell you a silver bullet. It was written to show you that the mortgage system isn't broken;

it's just built to benefit someone else. But when you understand how it works, you can flip the script.

You can cut years off your loan.

You can save tens of thousands in interest.

You can build wealth while reducing debt.

You can stop being a passenger and start being the driver.

Thanks for reading. I hope this book has helped you shift your mindset, sharpen your strategy, and take control of your financial future.

You're the boss now.

# About the Author

## Dave Hirst & Perch Finance

If you've made it this far, you're no longer playing the bank's game blind.

You understand how home loans actually work. You know the traps. You've got the tools to do something about it. The next step is putting it into action – and you don't have to do that alone.

That's where we come in. I run a mortgage broking business called *Perch Finance*, built around the same philosophy as this book: no gatekeeping, no hidden strategies, no $4,500 courses, and definitely no awkward weekend seminars ending in an investment property pitch. Just clear advice, smart loan structuring, and ongoing support to help you pay your loan off faster.

If you like the idea of open-sourcing finance – giving people the knowledge and tools to get ahead – then we'd love to help.

Visit perch.finance and reach out any time. Even if you just have a question, sing out.

And if you decide not to use us? No problem. Use the strategies in this book anyway. That's the whole point.

# About the Author

# Glossary

**Amortisation**

The process of paying off your loan over time through regular repayments.

At the start, most of your repayment goes to interest and barely touches the loan. Over time, that flips, and more goes toward reducing the balance.

**Annual Fee**

A once-a-year sting, usually tied to a home loan package.

**Application Fee**

The cost of asking the bank for money.

**Basic Loan**

No bells, no whistles, usually cheaper. Like a base-model car that gets the job done, but you have to wind the windows up manually.

**Borrower**

You. The one taking out the loan and paying all the interest.

**Capital Growth**

Increase in the property's value over time. The main game for most investors.

**Cash Flow**

How money moves in and out of your accounts. Control this, and everything else gets easier.

**Cash Rate**

The rate set by the RBA that influences all other interest rates.

**Comparison Rate**

The "true-ish" cost of a loan including some fees. Helpful, but also a bit like a movie trailer in that it doesn't show you everything.

**Compounding Interest**

Interest on interest. Amazing when you're earning it. Brutal when you're paying it.

**Daily Interest**

Interest is calculated every single day. Which means timing matters more than most people realise.

**Debt Recycling**

Turning non-deductible debt into deductible debt over time. Sounds complicated. It's not.

**Debt Reduction Strategy**

Your game plan for killing your loan faster.

**Deductibility**

Whether you can claim the interest as a tax deduction.

**Deposit**

Your upfront contribution. Proof you've got some skin in the game.

**Depreciation**

A paper deduction for wear and tear. You didn't spend the money, but you still get the tax benefit.

**Effective Balance**

Your loan balance minus your offset balance. The number the bank actually uses to calculate interest.

**Equity**

The portion of the property you own. The bank owns the rest (for now).

**Extra Repayments**

Paying more than required. Simple. Powerful. Underused.

**False Savings**

Earning 4% on savings while paying 6% on debt. Feels smart. It's not.

**Fixed Rate**

Locked-in interest rate that won't change during the fixed rate term. Stability, but with less flexibility.

**Gearing**

Borrowing to invest.

**Good Debt vs Bad Debt**

"Good debt" can be claimed for tax. "Bad debt" can't. (But let's be honest – it's all debt.)

**High-Interest Savings Account**

Like a regular savings account, but with slightly less disappointment.

**Home Loan**

The money the bank lends you to buy a property. Simple. You borrow it, you repay it (slowly), and you pay interest for the privilege.

**Interest**

The bank's cut for lending you money. It's like rent. The bank is temporarily lending you the money and in return, you pay them interest as a thank you.

**Interest Rate**

The percentage used to calculate how much the bank charges you. Small number, big consequences.

**Interest-Only**

You're only paying the interest each month, not reducing the loan. Great for cash flow. Terrible if you forget what's going on.

**Investment Property**
A property you rent out. Comes with income, expenses, and tax implications.

**Leveraging**
Using a small amount of your own money to control a much larger asset.

**Line of Credit**
An old loan type that behaves like a transaction account. Powerful, and dangerous if you don't know what you're doing.

**Loan Balance**
What you currently owe the bank. The number you wish would go down faster.

**Loan Limit**
The original amount you were approved for. Think of it as your "maximum damage" setting.

**Loan Purpose**
What the borrowed money is used for. Determines tax treatment.

**Loan Split**
Dividing a loan into parts for different purposes (often for tax strategy).

**Loan Structure**
How your loan and accounts are set up. Get this right and you save thousands. Get it wrong and the bank sends you a thank-you card.

**Loan Term**

How long the bank expects to keep you as a loyal customer (usually 30 years, unless you outsmart them).

**Marginal Tax Rate**

The rate of tax applied to your next dollar of income.

**Monthly Fee**

A regular reminder that banks love subscriptions too.

**Mortgage**

The literal meaning. Most people interchange “mortgage” with “home loan”. But it actually means the legal agreement that gives the bank rights over your property until the loan is repaid. If things go badly and you stop paying, the mortgage is what allows the bank to sell your home to get their money back. Fun fact: the word “mortgage” comes from Latin and literally means “death pledge.” Which feels dramatic, until you realise it sticks with you for 30 years and only dies when the debt does.

**Multiple Offset Accounts**

Several offset accounts for different purposes (bills, holidays, etc.). Great for organisation and mental accounting.

**Negative Gearing**

Your investment costs more than it earns. You lose money now to (hopefully) gain later.

**Neutral Gearing**

Break-even. Your investment property costs equal the income you get from it.

**Offset Account**

A transaction account linked to your loan that reduces the interest you're charged. Your money works for you instead of the bank.

**Owner-Occupied**

A home you live in. No tax perks, but also no landlord.

**P&I**

A repayment that pays the bank the interest plus a little more to reduce the balance of the loan.

**Parkinson's Law**

Money expands to fill the spending available. If it's there, it'll get spent.

**Positive Gearing**

Your investment earns more than it costs. The dream, until the tax bill arrives.

**Principal**

The actual money you borrowed. Not the bank's profit. (That comes later.)

**Professional Package**

A bundle of banking products with an annual fee. The bank's version of "value."

**Redraw Facility**

Extra repayments you've made that you can pull back out. Your money, but with a permission slip.

**Redraw Fees**

A fee to access your own money. Yes, really.

**Refinancing**

Breaking up with your current bank and moving in with a new one, usually for a better deal.

**Rental Yield**

How much income your property generates relative to its value.

**Repayment Frequency**

How often you pay your loan (monthly, fortnightly, etc.). Align it with your income and you'll get ahead faster.

**Repayments**

The least amount the bank will accept to keep them happy (and you in debt for longer).

**Reserve Bank of Australia**

The group that moves interest rates and keeps mortgage holders on their toes.

**Savings Account**

Where money is supposed to grow. Slowly, very slowly.

**Security**

The asset (usually your home) the bank can sell if things go sideways.

**Stamp Duty**

A state government tax on buying property. First home buyers usually get a good discount, while investors pay the full rate.

**Tax-Deduction**

An expense you can claim to reduce your taxable income. The tax man's version of a discount.

**Term Deposit**

Lock your money away for a fixed time in exchange for a fixed rate. Great if you enjoy not touching your own cash.

**Transaction Account**

Your everyday spending account. Also known as "where money goes to disappear."

**Variable Rate**

Interest rate that moves with the market. Flexibility with uncertainty.

www.ingramcontent.com/pod-product-compliance
Lightning Source LLC
La Vergne TN
LVHW052323200926
848481LV00002B/656
* 9 7 8 1 7 6 4 7 2 5 8 0 4 *